PENGUIN BOOKS — GREAT IDEAS

On the Shortness of Life

Seneca

c. 5 BC—AD 65

Seneca

On the Shortness of Life

TRANSLATED BY C. D. N. COSTA

PENGUIN BOOKS — GREAT IDEAS

PENGUIN BOOKS

Published by the Penguin Group
Penguin Books Ltd, 80 Strand, London WC2R ORL, England
Penguin Group (USA) Inc., 375 Hudson Street, New York, New York 10014, USA
Penguin Books Australia Ltd, 250 Camberwell Road,
Camberwell, Victoria 3124, Australia
Penguin Books Canada Ltd, 10 Alcorn Avenue, Toronto, Ontario, Canada M4V 3B2
Penguin Books India (P) Ltd, 11 Community Centre,
Panchsheel Park, New Delhi – 110 017, India
Penguin Group (NZ), Cnr Airborne and Rosedale Roads,
Albany, Auckland 1310, New Zealand
Penguin Books (South Africa) (Pty) Ltd, 24 Sturdee Avenue,
Rosebank 2196, South Africa

Penguin Books Ltd, Registered Offices: 80 Strand, London WC2R ORL, England

www.penguin.com

First published in *Dialogues and Letters* in Penguin Classics 1997
This selection first published in Penguin Books 2004

14

Taken from the Penguin Classics edition *Dialogues and Letters*,
translated and edited by C. D. N. Costa

Set in Monotype Dante
Typeset by Rowland Phototypesetting Ltd, Bury St Edmunds, Suffolk
Printed in England by Clays Ltd, St Ives plc

ISBN-13: 978–0–141–01881–2

www.greenpenguin.co.uk

Contents

On the Shortness of Life

Most human beings, Paulinus,* complain about the meanness of nature, because we are born for a brief span of life, and because this spell of time that has been given to us rushes by so swiftly and rapidly that with very few exceptions life ceases for the rest of us just when we are getting ready for it. Nor is it just the man in the street and the unthinking mass of people who groan over this – as they see it – universal evil: the same feeling lies behind complaints from even distinguished men. Hence the dictum of the greatest of doctors:† 'Life is short, art is long.' Hence too the grievance, most improper to a wise man, which Aristotle expressed when he was taking nature to task for indulging animals with such long existences that they can live through five or ten human lifetimes, while a far shorter limit is set for men who are born to a great and extensive destiny. It is not that we have a short time to live, but that we waste a lot of it. Life is long enough, and a sufficiently generous amount has been given to us for the highest achievements if it were all well invested. But when it is wasted in heedless luxury and spent on no good activity, we are forced at last by death's final constraint to realize that it has passed

* A friend of Seneca's.
† Hippocrates.

I

away before we knew it was passing. So it is: we are not given a short life but we make it short, and we are not ill-supplied but wasteful of it. Just as when ample and princely wealth falls to a bad owner it is squandered in a moment, but wealth however modest, if entrusted to a good custodian, increases with use, so our lifetime extends amply if you manage it properly.

Why do we complain about nature? She has acted kindly: life is long if you know how to use it. But one man is gripped by insatiable greed, another by a laborious dedication to useless tasks. One man is soaked in wine, another sluggish with idleness. One man is worn out by political ambition, which is always at the mercy of the judgement of others. Another through hope of profit is driven headlong over all lands and seas by the greed of trading. Some are tormented by a passion for army life, always intent on inflicting dangers on others or anxious about danger to themselves. Some are worn out by the self-imposed servitude of thankless attendance on the great. Many are occupied by either pursuing other people's money or complaining about their own. Many pursue no fixed goal, but are tossed about in ever-changing designs by a fickleness which is shifting, in-constant and never satisfied with itself. Some have no aims at all for their life's course, but death takes them unawares as they yawn languidly – so much so that I cannot doubt the truth of that oracular remark of the greatest of poets: 'It is a small part of life we really live.' Indeed, all the rest is not life but merely time. Vices surround and assail men from every side, and do not allow them to rise again and lift their eyes to discern the truth, but keep them overwhelmed and rooted in their desires. Never can they recover their true selves. If by chance they achieve some tranquillity, just as a swell remains on the deep sea even after the wind has dropped, so they go on tossing about and never find rest from their desires. Do you think I am speaking only of those whose wickedness is acknowledged? Look at those whose good fortune people gather to see: they are choked by their own blessings. How many find their riches a burden! How many burst a blood vessel by their eloquence and their daily striving to show off their talents! How many are pale from constant pleasures! How many are left no freedom by the crowd of clients surrounding them! In a word, run through them all, from lowest to highest: one calls for legal assistance, another comes to help; one is on trial, another defends him, another gives a judgment; no one makes his claim to himself, but each is exploited for another's sake. Ask about those whose names are learned by heart, and you will see that they have these distinguishing marks: X cultivates Y and Y cultivates Z – no one bothers about himself. Again, certain people reveal the most stupid indignation: they complain about the pride of their superiors because they did not have time to give them an audience when they wanted one. But can anyone dare to complain about another's pride when he himself never has time for himself? Yet whoever you are, the great man has sometimes gazed upon you, even if his look was patronizing, he has bent his ears to your words, he has let you walk beside him. But you never deign to look at yourself or listen to yourself. So you have no reason to claim credit from anyone for those attentions, since you showed them not because you wanted someone else's company but because you could not bear your own.

Even if all the bright intellects who ever lived were to agree to ponder this one theme, they would never sufficiently express their surprise at this fog in the human mind. Men do not let anyone seize their estates, and if there is the slightest dispute about their boundaries they rush to stones and arms; but they allow others to encroach on their lives – why, they themselves even invite in those who will take over their lives. You will find no one willing to share out his money; but to how many does each of us divide up his life! People are frugal in guarding their personal property; but as soon as it comes to squandering time they are most wasteful of the one thing in which it is right to be stingy. So, I would like to fasten on someone from the older generation and say to him: 'I see that you have come to the last stage of human life; you are close upon your hundredth year, or even beyond: come now, hold an audit of your life. Reckon how much of your time has been taken up by a money-lender, how much by a mistress, a patron, a client, quarrelling with your wife, punishing your slaves, dashing about the city on your social obligations. Consider also the diseases which we have brought on ourselves, and the time too which has been unused. You will find that you have fewer years than you reckon. Call to mind when you ever had a fixed purpose; how few days have passed as you had planned; when you were ever at your own disposal; when your face wore its natural expression; when your mind was undisturbed;

what work you have achieved in such a long life; how many have plundered your life when you were unaware of your losses; how much you have lost through ground-less sorrow, foolish joy, greedy desire, the seductions of society; how little of your own was left to you. You will realize that you are dying prematurely.'

So what is the reason for this? You are living as if destined to live for ever; your own frailty never occurs to you; you don't notice how much time has already passed, but squander it as though you had a full and overflowing supply – though all the while that very day which you are devoting to somebody or something may be your last. You act like mortals in all that you fear, and like immortals in all that you desire. You will hear many people saying: 'When I am fifty I shall retire into leisure; when I am sixty I shall give up public duties.' And what guarantee do you have of a longer life? Who will allow your course to proceed as you arrange it? Aren't you ashamed to keep for yourself just the remnants of your life, and to devote to wisdom only that time which cannot be spent on any business? How late it is to begin really to live just when life must end! How stupid to forget our mortality, and put off sensible plans to our fiftieth and sixtieth years, aiming to begin life from a point at which few have arrived!

You will notice that the most powerful and highly stationed men let drop remarks in which they pray for leisure, praise it, and rate it higher than all their blessings. At times they long to descend from their pinnacles if they can in safety; for even if nothing external assails or agitates it, high fortune of itself comes crashing down.

The deified Augustus, to whom the gods granted more than to anyone else, never ceased to pray for rest and to seek a respite from public affairs. Everything he said always reverted to this theme – his hope for leisure. He used to beguile his labours with this consolation, sweet though false, that one day he would live to please himself. In a letter he wrote to the senate, after he promised that his rest would not be lacking in dignity nor inconsistent with his former glory, I find these words: 'But it is more impressive to carry out these things than to promise them. Nevertheless, since the delightful reality is still a long way off, my longing for that much desired time has led me to anticipate some of its delight by the pleasure arising from words.' So valuable did leisure seem to him that because he could not enjoy it in actuality, he did so mentally in advance. He who saw that everything depended on himself alone, who decided the fortune of individuals and nations, was happiest when thinking of that day on which he would lay aside his own greatness. He knew from experience how much sweat those blessings gleaming through every land cost him, how many secret anxieties they concealed. He was forced to fight first with his fellow-countrymen, then with his colleagues, and finally with his relations, shedding blood on land and sea. Driven to fight in Macedonia, Sicily, Egypt, Syria, Asia – almost every country – he turned his armies against foreign enemies when they were tired of shedding Roman blood. While he was establishing peace in the Alps and subduing enemies established in the middle of his peaceful empire; while he was extending his boundaries beyond the Rhine, the Euphrates and the Danube, at Rome itself Murena, Caepio, Lepidus, Egnatius and others were sharpening their swords against him. Nor had he yet escaped their plots when his daughter and all the noble youths bound to her by adultery as though by an oath kept alarming his feeble old age, as did Iullus and a second formidable woman linked to an Antony. He cut away these ulcers, limbs and all, but others took their place: just like a body with a surfeit of blood which is always subject to a haemorrhage somewhere. So he longed for leisure, and as his hopes and thoughts dwelt on that he found relief for his labours: this was the prayer of the man who could grant the prayers of mankind.

When Marcus Cicero was cast among men like Catiline and Clodius and Pompey and Crassus – some of them undisguised enemies and some doubtful friends – when he was tossed about in the storm that struck the state, he tried to hold it steady as it went to its doom; but at last he was swept away. He had neither peace in prosperity nor patience in adversity, and how often does he curse that very consulship, which he had praised without ceasing though not without good reason! What woeful words he uses in a letter to Atticus when the elder Pompey had been conquered, and his son was still trying to revive his defeated forces in Spain! 'Do you want to know,' he said, 'what I am doing here? I am staying a semi-prisoner in my Tusculan villa.' He then goes on to bewail his former life, to complain of the present, and to despair of the future. Cicero called himself a semi-prisoner, but really and truly the wise man will never go so far as to use such an abject term. He will never be a semi-prisoner, but will always enjoy freedom which is solid and complete, at liberty to be his own master and higher than all others. For what can be above the man who is above fortune?

Livius Drusus, a bold and vigorous man, had proposed laws which renewed the evil policy of the Gracchi, and he was supported by a huge crowd from all over Italy. But he could see no successful outcome for his measures, which he could neither carry through nor abandon once embarked upon; and he is said to have cursed the turbulent life he had always lived, saying that he alone had never had a holiday even as a child. For while still a ward and dressed as a youth he ventured to speak to a jury in favour of some accused men, and to acquire influence in the law courts, with so much effect that, as we all know, he forced certain verdicts favourable to his clients. To what lengths would so precocious an ambition not go? You might have known that such premature boldness would result in terrible trouble, both public and private. So he was too late in complaining that he had never had a holiday, since from his boyhood he had been a serious trouble-maker in the Forum. It is uncertain whether he died by his own hand, for he collapsed after receiving a sudden wound in the groin, some people doubting whether his death was self-inflicted, but no one doubting that it was timely.

It would be superfluous to mention any more who, though seeming to others the happiest of mortals, themselves bore true witness against themselves by their expressed hatred of every action of their lives. Yet they did not change themselves or anyone else by these complaints, for after their explosion of words their feelings reverted to normal.

Assuredly your lives, even if they last more than a thousand years, will shrink into the tiniest span: those vices will swallow up any space of time. The actual time you have – which reason can prolong though it naturally passes quickly – inevitably escapes you rapidly: for you do not grasp it or hold it back or try to delay that swiftest of all things, but you let it slip away as though it were something superfluous and replaceable.

But among the worst offenders I count those who spend all their time in drinking and lust, for these are the worst preoccupations of all. Other people, even if they are possessed by an illusory semblance of glory, suffer from a respectable delusion. You can give me a list of miserly men, or hot-tempered men who indulge in unjust hatreds or wars: but they are all sinning in a more manly way. It is those who are on a headlong course of gluttony and lust who are stained with dishonour. Examine how all these people spend their time – how long they devote to their accounts, to laying traps for others or fearing those laid for themselves, to paying court to others or being courted themselves, to giving or receiving bail, to banquets (which now count as official business): you will see how their activities, good or bad, do not give them even time to breathe.

Finally, it is generally agreed that no activity can be successfully pursued by an individual who is preoccupied – not rhetoric or liberal studies – since the mind when distracted absorbs nothing deeply, but rejects everything which is, so to speak, crammed into it. Living is the least important activity of the preoccupied man; yet there is nothing which is harder to learn. There are many instructors in the other arts to be found everywhere: indeed, some of these arts mere boys have grasped so thoroughly that they can even teach them. But learning how to live takes a whole life, and, which may surprise you more, it takes a whole life to learn how to die. So many of the finest men have put aside all their encumbrances, renouncing riches and business and pleasure, and made it their one aim up to the end of their lives to know how to live. Yet most of these have died confessing that they did not yet know – still less can those others know. Believe me, it is the sign of a great man, and one who is above human error, not to allow his time to be frittered away: he has the longest possible life simply because whatever time was available he devoted entirely to himself. None of it lay fallow and neglected, none of it under another's control; for being an extremely thrifty guardian of his time he never found anything for which it was worth exchanging. So he had enough time; but those into whose lives the public have made great inroads inevitably have too little.

Nor must you think that such people do not sometimes recognize their loss. Indeed, you will hear many of those to whom great prosperity is a burden sometimes crying out amidst their hordes of clients or their pleadings in law courts or their other honourable miseries. 'It's impossible to live.' Of course it's impossible. All those who call you to themselves draw you away from yourself. How many days has that defendant stolen from you? Or that candidate? Or that old lady worn out with burying her heirs? Or that man shamming an illness to excite the greed of legacy-hunters? Or that influential friend who keeps people like you not for friendship but for display? Mark off, I tell you, and review the days of your life: you will see that very few – the useless remnants – have been left to you. One man who has achieved the badge of office he coveted longs to lay it aside, and keeps repeating, 'Will this year never end?' Another man thought it a great coup to win the chance of giving games, but, having given them, he says, 'When shall I be rid of them?' That advocate is grabbed on every side throughout the Forum, and fills the whole place with a huge crowd extending further than he can be heard: but he says, 'When will vacation come?' Everyone hustles his life along, and is troubled by a longing for the future and weariness of the present. But the man who spends all his time on his own needs, who organizes every day as though it were his last, neither longs for nor fears the next day. For what new pleasures can any hour now bring him? He has tried everything, and enjoyed everything to repletion. For the rest, Fortune can dispose as she likes: his life is now secure. Nothing can be taken from this life, and you can only add to it as if giving to a man who is already full and satisfied food which he does not want but can hold. So you must not think a man has lived long because he has white hair and wrinkles: he has not lived long, just existed long. For suppose you should think that a man had had a long voyage who had been caught in a raging storm as he left harbour, and carried hither and thither and driven round and round in a circle by the rage of opposing winds? He did not have a long voyage, just a long tossing about.

I am always surprised to see some people demanding the time of others and meeting a most obliging response. Both sides have in view the reason for which the time is asked and neither regards the time itself – as if nothing there is being asked for and nothing given. They are trifling with life's most precious commodity, being deceived because it is an intangible thing, not open to inspection and therefore reckoned very cheap – in fact, almost without any value. People are delighted to accept pensions and gratuities, for which they hire out their labour or their support or their services. But nobody works out the value of time: men use it lavishly as if it cost nothing. But if death threatens these same people, you will see them praying to their doctors; if they are in fear of capital punishment, you will see them prepared to spend their all to stay alive. So inconsistent are they in their feelings. But if each of us could have the tally of his future years set before him, as we can of our past years, how alarmed would be those who saw only a few years ahead, and how carefully would they use them! And yet it is easy to organize an amount, however small, which is assured; we have to be more careful in preserving what will cease at an unknown point.

But you are not to think that these people do not know how precious time is. They commonly say to those they are particularly fond of that they are ready to give them some of their years. And they do give them without being aware of it; but the gift is such that they themselves lose without adding anything to the others. But what they actually do not know is whether they are losing; thus they can bear the loss of what they do not know has gone. No one will bring back the years; no one will restore you to yourself. Life will follow the path it began to take, and will neither reverse nor check its course. It will cause no commotion to remind you of its swiftness, but glide on quietly. It will not lengthen itself for a king's command or a people's favour. As it started out on its first day, so it will run on, nowhere pausing or turning aside. What will be the outcome? You have been preoccupied while life hastens on. Meanwhile death will arrive, and you have no choice in making yourself available for that.

Can anything be more idiotic than certain people who boast of their foresight? They keep themselves officiously preoccupied in order to improve their lives; they spend their lives in organizing their lives. They direct their purposes with an eye to a distant future. But putting things off is the biggest waste of life: it snatches away each day as it comes, and denies us the present by promising the future. The greatest obstacle to living is expectancy, which hangs upon tomorrow and loses today. You are arranging what lies in Fortune's control, and abandoning what lies in yours. What are you looking at? To what goal are you straining? The whole future lies in uncertainty: live immediately. Listen to the cry of our greatest poet, who as though inspired with divine utterance sings salutary verses:

> Life's finest day for wretched mortals here
> Is always first to flee.

'Why do you linger?' he means. 'Why are you idle? If you don't grasp it first, it flees.' And even if you do grasp it, it will still flee. So you must match time's swiftness with your speed in using it, and you must drink quickly as though from a rapid stream that will not always flow. In chastising endless delay, too, the poet very elegantly speaks not of the 'finest age' but 'finest day'. However greedy you are, why are you so unconcerned and so sluggish (while time flies so fast), extending months and years in a long sequence ahead of you? The poet is telling you about the day – and about this very day that is escaping. So can it be doubted that for wretched mortals – that is, the preoccupied – the finest day is always the first to flee? Old age overtakes them while they are still mentally childish, and they face it unprepared and unarmed. For they have made no provision for it, stumbling upon it suddenly and unawares, and without realizing that it was approaching day by day. Just as travellers are beguiled by conversation or reading or some profound meditation, and find they have arrived at their destination before they knew they were approaching it; so it is with this unceasing and extremely fast-moving journey of life, which waking or sleeping we make at the same pace – the preoccupied become aware of it only when it is over.

If I wanted to divide my theme into different headings and offer proofs, I would find many arguments to prove that the preoccupied find life very short. But Fabianus, who was not one of today's academic philosophers but the true old-fashioned sort, used to say that we must attack the passions by brute force and not by logic; that the enemy's line must be turned by a strong attack and not by pinpricks; for vices have to be crushed rather than picked at. Still, in order that the people concerned may be censured for their own individual faults, they must be taught and not just given up for lost.

Life is divided into three periods, past, present and future. Of these, the present is short, the future is doubtful, the past is certain. For this last is the one over which Fortune has lost her power, which cannot be brought back to anyone's control. But this is what preoccupied people lose: for they have no time to look back at their past, and even if they did, it is not pleasant to recall activities they are ashamed of. So they are unwilling to cast their minds back to times ill spent, which they dare not relive if their vices in recollection become obvious – even those vices whose insidious approach was disguised by the charm of some momentary pleasure. No one willingly reverts to the past unless all his actions have passed his own censorship, which is never deceived. The man who must fear his own memory is the one who has been ambitious in his greed, arrogant in his contempt, uncontrolled in his victories, treacherous in his deceptions, rapacious in his plundering, and wasteful in his squandering. And yet this is the period of our time which is sacred and dedicated, which has passed beyond all human risks and is removed from Fortune's sway, which cannot be harassed by want or fear or attacks of illness. It cannot be disturbed or snatched from us: it is an untroubled, everlasting possession. In the present we have only one day at a time, each offering a minute at a time. But all the days of the past will come to your call:

you can detain and inspect them at your will – something which the preoccupied have no time to do. It is the mind which is tranquil and free from care which can roam through all the stages of its life: the minds of the preoccupied, as if harnessed in a yoke, cannot turn round and look behind them. So their lives vanish into an abyss; and just as it is no use pouring any amount of liquid into a container without a bottom to catch and hold it, so it does not matter how much time we are given if there is nowhere for it to settle; it escapes through the cracks and holes of the mind. The present time is extremely short, so much so that some people are unaware of it. For it is always on the move, flowing on in a rush; it ceases before it has come, and does not suffer delay any more than the firmament or the stars, whose unceasing movement never pauses in the same place. And so the preoccupied are concerned only with the present, and it is so short that it cannot be grasped, and even this is stolen from them while they are involved in their many distractions.

In a word, would you like to know how they do not live long? See how keen they are to live long. Feeble old men pray for a few more years; they pretend they are younger than they are; they comfort themselves by this deception and fool themselves as eagerly as if they fooled Fate at the same time. But when at last some illness has reminded them of their mortality, how terrified do they die, as if they were not just passing out of life but being dragged out of it. They exclaim that they were fools because they have not really lived, and that if only they can recover from this illness they will live in leisure.

Then they reflect how pointlessly they acquired things they never would enjoy, and how all their toil has been in vain. But for those whose life is far removed from all business it must be amply long. None of it is frittered away, none of it scattered here and there, none of it committed to fortune, none of it lost through carelessness, none of it wasted on largesse, none of it superfluous: the whole of it, so to speak, is well invested. So, however short, it is fully sufficient, and therefore whenever his last day comes, the wise man will not hesitate to meet death with a firm step.

Perhaps you want to know whom I would call the preoccupied? You must not imagine I mean just those who are driven from the law court only by the arrival of the watchdogs; or those whom you see crushed either honourably in their own crowd of supporters or contemptuously in someone else's; or those whose social duties bring them forth from their own homes to dash them against someone else's doors; or those whom the praetor's auction spear occupies in acquiring disreputable gain which will one day turn rank upon them. Some men are preoccupied even in their leisure: in their country house, on their couch, in the midst of solitude, even when quite alone, they are their own worst company. You could not call theirs a life of leisure, but an idle preoccupation. Do you call that man leisured who arranges with anxious precision his Corinthian bronzes, the cost of which is inflated by the mania of a few collectors, and spends most of the day on rusty bits of metal? Who sits at a wrestling ring (for shame on us! We suffer from vices which are not even Roman), keenly following the bouts between boys? Who classifies his herds of pack-animals into pairs according to age and colour? Who pays for the maintenance of the latest athletes? Again, do you call those men leisured who spend many hours at the barber's simply to cut whatever grew overnight, to have a serious debate about every separate hair, to tidy up disarranged locks or to train thinning ones from the sides to lie over the forehead? How angry they get if the barber has been a bit careless – as if he were trimming a real man! How they flare up if any of their mane is wrongly cut off, if any of it is badly arranged, or if it doesn't all fall into the right ringlets! Which of them would not rather have his country ruffled than his hair? Which would not be more anxious about the elegance of his head than its safety? Which would not rather be trim than honourable? Do you call those men leisured who divide their time between the comb and the mirror? And what about those who busy themselves in composing, listening to, or learning songs, while they distort their voice, whose best and simplest tone nature intended to be the straight one, into the most unnatural modulations; who are always drumming with their fingers as they beat time to an imagined tune; whom you can hear humming to themselves even when they are summoned on a serious, often even sorrowful, affair? Theirs is not leisure but indolent occupation. And, good heavens, as for their banquets, I would not reckon on them as leisure times when I see how anxiously they arrange their silver, how carefully they gird up the tunics of their page-boys, how on tenterhooks they are to see how the cook has dealt with the boar, with what speed smooth-faced slaves rush around on their duties, with what skill birds are carved into appropriate portions, how carefully wretched little slaves wipe up the spittle of drunkards. By these means they cultivate a reputation for elegance and good taste, and to such an extent do their failings follow them into all areas of their private lives that they cannot eat or drink without ostentation.

I would also not count as leisured those who are carried around in a sedan chair and a litter, and turn up punctually for their drives as if it was forbidden to give them up; who have to be told when to bathe or to swim or to dine: they are so enervated by the excessive torpor of a self-indulgent mind that they cannot trust themselves to know if they are hungry. I am told that one of these self-indulgent people – if self-indulgence is the right word for unlearning the ordinary habits of human life – when he had been carried out from the bath and put in his sedan chair, asked, 'Am I now sitting down?' Do you think that this man, who doesn't know if he is sitting down, knows whether he is alive, whether he sees, whether he is at leisure? It is difficult to say whether I pity him more if he really did not know this or if he pretended not to know. They really experience forgetfulness of many things, but they also pretend to forget many things. They take delight in certain vices as proofs of their good fortune: it seems to be the lowly and contemptible man who knows what he is doing. After that see if you can accuse the mimes of inventing many details in order to attack luxury! In truth, they pass over more than they make up, and such a wealth of incredible vices have appeared in this generation, which shows talent in this one area, that we could now actually accuse the mimes of ignoring them. To think that there is anyone so lost in luxuries that he has to trust another to tell him if he is sitting down! So this one is not at leisure, and you must give him another description – he is ill, or even, he is dead: the man who is really at leisure is also aware of it. But this one who is only half alive, and needs to be told the positions of his own body – how can he have control over any of his time?

It would be tedious to mention individually those who have spent all their lives playing draughts or ball, or carefully cooking themselves in the sun. They are not at leisure whose pleasures involve a serious commitment. For example, nobody will dispute that those people are busy about nothing who spend their time on useless literary studies: even among the Romans there is now a large company of these. It used to be a Greek failing to want to know how many oarsmen Ulysses had, whether the *Iliad* or the *Odyssey* was written first, and whether too they were by the same author, and other questions of this kind, which if you keep them to yourself in no way enhance your private knowledge, and if you publish them make you appear more a bore than a scholar. But now the Romans too have been afflicted by the pointless enthusiasm for useless knowledge. Recently I heard somebody reporting which Roman general first did this or that: Duilius first won a naval battle; Curius Dentatus first included elephants in a triumph. So far these facts, even if they do not contribute to real glory, at least are concerned with exemplary services to the state: such knowledge will not do us any good, but it interests us because of the appeal of these pointless facts. We can also excuse those who investigate who first persuaded the Romans to embark on a ship. That was Claudius, who for this reason was called Caudex because a structure linking several wooden planks was called in antiquity a *caudex*. Hence too the Law Tables are called *codices*, and even today the boats which carry provisions up the Tiber are called by the old-fashioned name *codicariae*. Doubtless too it is of some importance to know that Valerius Corvinus first conquered Messana, and was the first of the family of the Valerii to be surnamed Messana from the name of the captured city – the spelling of which was gradually corrupted in everyday speech to Messalla. Perhaps you will also allow someone to take seriously the fact that Lucius Sulla first exhibited lions loose in the Circus, though at other times they were shown in fetters, and that javelin-throwers were sent by King Bocchus to kill them. This too may be excused – but does it serve any good purpose? – to know that Pompey first exhibited in the Circus a fight involving eighteen elephants, pitting innocent men against them in a staged battle. A leader of the state and, as we are told, a man of notable kindliness among the leaders of old, he thought it would be a memorable spectacle to kill human beings in a novel way. 'Are they to fight to the death? Not good enough. Are they to be torn to pieces? Not good enough. Let them be crushed by animals of enormous bulk.' It would be better for such things to be forgotten, lest in the future someone in power might learn about them and not wish to be outdone in such a piece of inhumanity. Oh, what darkness does great prosperity cast over our minds! He thought himself beyond nature's laws at the time that he was throwing so many crowds of wretched men to wild creatures from abroad, when he was setting such disparate creatures against each other, when he was shedding so much blood in front of the Roman people, who themselves were soon to be forced by him to shed their own blood. But later he himself, betrayed by Alexandrian treachery, offered himself to be stabbed by the lowest slave, only then realizing that his surname ('Great') was an empty boast.

But to return to the point from which I digressed, and to illustrate how some people spend useless efforts on these same topics, the man I referred to reported that Metellus in his triumph, after conquering the Carthaginians in Sicily, alone among all the Romans had 120 elephants led before his chariot, and that Sulla was the last of the Romans to have extended the *pomerium*,* which it was the ancient practice to extend after acquiring Italian, but never provincial, territory. Is it better to know this than to know that the Aventine Hill, as he asserted, is outside the *pomerium* for one of two reasons, either because the plebs withdrew to it or because when Remus took the auspices there the birds had not been favourable – and countless further theories that are either false or very close to lies? For even if you admit that they say all this in good faith, even if they guarantee the truth of their statements, whose mistakes will thereby be lessened? Whose passions restrained? Who will be made more free, more just, more magnanimous? Our Fabianus

---

* The religious boundary of a city.

used to say that sometimes he wondered whether it was better not to be involved in any researches than to get entangled in these.

Of all people only those are at leisure who make time for philosophy, only those are really alive. For they not only keep a good watch over their own lifetimes, but they annex every age to theirs. All the years that have passed before them are added to their own. Unless we are very ungrateful, all those distinguished founders of holy creeds were born for us and prepared for us a way of life. By the toil of others we are led into the presence of things which have been brought from darkness into light. We are excluded from no age, but we have access to them all; and if we are prepared in loftiness of mind to pass beyond the narrow confines of human weakness, there is a long period of time through which we can roam. We can argue with Socrates, express doubt with Carneades, cultivate retirement with Epicurus, overcome human nature with the Stoics, and exceed its limits with the Cynics. Since nature allows us to enter into a partnership with every age, why not turn from this brief and transient spell of time and give ourselves wholeheartedly to the past, which is limitless and eternal and can be shared with better men than we?

Those who rush about on social duties, disturbing both themselves and others, when they have duly finished their crazy round and have daily crossed everyone's threshold and passed by no open door, when they have carried around their self-interested greetings to houses that are miles apart, how few will they be able to see in a city so enormous and so distracted by varied desires? How many will there be who through sleepiness or self-indulgence or ungraciousness will exclude them? How many, after keeping them in an agony of waiting, will pretend to be in a hurry and rush past them? How many will avoid going out through a hall crowded with dependants, and escape through a secret door – as if it were not even more discourteous to deceive callers than to exclude them? How many, half asleep and sluggish after yesterday's drinking, will yawn insolently and have to be prompted a thousand times in a whisper before, scarcely moving their lips, they can greet by name the poor wretches who have broken their own slumbers in order to wait on another's?

You should rather suppose that those are involved in worthwhile duties who wish to have daily as their closest friends Zeno, Pythagoras, Democritus and all the other high priests of liberal studies, and Aristotle and Theophrastus. None of these will be too busy to see you, none of these will not send his visitor away happier and more devoted to himself, none of these will allow anyone to depart empty-handed. They are at home to all mortals by night and by day.

None of these will force you to die, but all will teach you how to die. None of them will exhaust your years, but each will contribute his years to yours. With none of these will conversation be dangerous, or his friendship fatal, or attendance on him expensive. From them you can take whatever you wish: it will not be their fault if you do not take your fill from them. What happiness, what a fine old age awaits the man who has made himself a client of these! He will have friends whose advice he can ask on the most important or the most trivial matters, whom he can consult daily about himself, who will tell him the truth without insulting him and praise him without flattery, who will offer him a pattern on which to model himself.

We are in the habit of saying that it was not in our power to choose the parents who were allotted to us, that they were given to us by chance. But we can choose whose children we would like to be. There are households of the noblest intellects: choose the one into which you wish to be adopted, and you will inherit not only their name but their property too. Nor will this property need to be guarded meanly or grudgingly: the more it is shared out, the greater it will become. These will offer you a path to immortality and raise you to a point from which no one is cast down. This is the only way to prolong mortality – even to convert it to immortality. Honours, monuments, whatever the ambitious have ordered by decrees or raised in public buildings are soon destroyed: there is nothing that the passage of time does not demolish and remove. But it cannot damage the works which philosophy has consecrated: no age will wipe them out, no age diminish them. The next and every following age will only increase the veneration for them, since envy operates on what is at hand, but we can more openly admire things from a distance. So the life of the philosopher extends widely: he is not confined by the same boundary as are others. He alone is free from the laws that limit the human race, and all ages serve him as though he were a god. Some time has passed: he grasps it in his recollection. Time is present:

he uses it. Time is to come: he anticipates it. This combination of all times into one gives him a long life.

But life is very short and anxious for those who forget the past, neglect the present, and fear the future. When they come to the end of it, the poor wretches realize too late that for all this time they have been preoccupied in doing nothing. And the fact that they sometimes invoke death is no proof that their lives seem long. Their own folly afflicts them with restless emotions which hurl themselves upon the very things they fear: they often long for death because they fear it. Nor is this a proof that they are living for a long time that the day often seems long to them, or that they complain that the hours pass slowly until the time fixed for dinner arrives. For as soon as their preoccupations fail them, they are restless with nothing to do, not knowing how to dispose of their leisure or make the time pass. And so they are anxious for something else to do, and all the intervening time is wearisome: really, it is just as when a gladiatorial show has been announced, or they are looking forward to the appointed time of some other exhibition or amusement – they want to leap over the days in between. Any deferment of the longed-for event is tedious to them. Yet the time of the actual enjoyment is short and swift, and made much shorter through their own fault. For they dash from one pleasure to another and cannot stay steady in one desire. Their days are not long but odious: on the other hand, how short do the nights seem which they spend drinking or sleeping with harlots! Hence the lunacy of the poets, who encourage human frailty by their stories in which Jupiter, seduced by the pleasures of love-making, is seen to double the length of the night. What else is it but to inflame our vices when they quote the gods to endorse them, and as a precedent for our failings they offer – and excuse – the wantonness of the gods? Can the nights, which they purchase so dearly, not seem much too short to these people? They lose the day in waiting for the night, and the night in fearing the dawn.

Even their pleasures are uneasy and made anxious by various fears, and at the very height of their rejoicing the worrying thought steals over them: 'How long will this last?' This feeling has caused kings to bewail their power, and they were not so much delighted by the greatness of their fortune as terrified by the thought of its inevitable end. When that most arrogant king of Persia* was deploying his army over vast plains, and could not number it but had to measure it, he wept because in a hundred years out of that huge army not a soul would be alive. But he who was weeping was the very man who would bring their fate upon them, and would destroy some on the sea, some on land, some in battle, some in flight, and in a very short time would wipe out all those for whose hundredth year he was afraid.

And what of the fact that even their joys are uneasy? The reason is that they are not based on firm causes, but they are agitated as groundlessly as they arise. But what kind of times can those be, do you think, which they themselves admit are wretched, since even the joys by

* Xerxes.

which they are exalted and raised above humanity are pretty corrupt? All the greatest blessings create anxiety, and Fortune is never less to be trusted than when it is fairest. To preserve prosperity we need other prosperity, and to support the prayers which have turned out well we have to make other prayers. Whatever comes our way by chance is unsteady, and the higher it rises the more liable it is to fall. Furthermore, what is doomed to fall delights no one. So it is inevitable that life will be not just very short but very miserable for those who acquire by great toil what they must keep by greater toil. They achieve what they want laboriously; they possess what they have achieved anxiously; and meanwhile they take no account of time that will never more return. New preoccupations take the place of the old, hope excites more hope and ambition more ambition. They do not look for an end to their misery, but simply change the reason for it. We have found our own public honours a torment, and we spend more time on someone else's. We have stopped labouring as candidates, and we start canvassing for others. We have given up the troubles of a prosecutor, and taken on those of a judge. A man stops being a judge and becomes president of a court. He has grown old in the job of managing the property of others for a salary, and then spends all his time looking after his own. Marius was released from army life to become busy in the consulship. Quintius hastens to get through his dictatorship, but he will be summoned back to it from the plough. Scipio will go against the Carthaginians before he is experienced enough for such an undertaking. Victorious over Hannibal, victorious over Antiochus, distinguished in his own consulship and a surety for his brother's, if he had not himself forbidden it he would have been set up beside Jupiter. But discord in the state will harass its saviour, and after as a young man he has scorned honours fit for the gods, at length when old he will take delight in an ostentatiously stubborn exile. There will always be causes for anxiety, whether due to prosperity or to wretchedness. Life will be driven on through a succession of preoccupations: we shall always long for leisure, but never enjoy it.

And so, my dear Paulinus, extract yourself from the crowd, and as you have been storm-tossed more than your age deserves, you must at last retire into a peaceful harbour. Consider how many waves you have encountered, how many storms – some of which you have sustained in private life and some you have brought upon yourself in public life. Your virtue has for long enough been shown, when you were a model of active industry: try how it will manage in leisure. The greater part of your life, certainly the better part, has been devoted to the state: take some of your own time for yourself too. I am not inviting you to idle or purposeless sloth, or to drown all your natural energy in sleep and the pleasures that are dear to the masses. That is not to have repose. When you are retired and enjoying peace of mind, you will find to keep you busy more important activities than all those you have performed so energetically up to now. Indeed, you are managing the accounts of the world as scrupulously as you would another person's, as carefully as your own, as conscientiously as the state's. You are winning affection in a job in which it is hard to avoid ill-will; but believe me it is better to understand the balance-sheet of one's own life than of the corn trade. You must recall that vigorous mind of yours, supremely capable of dealing with the greatest responsibilities, from a task which is certainly honourable but scarcely suited to the happy life; and you must consider that all your youthful training in the liberal studies was not directed to this end, that many thousands of measures of corn might safely be entrusted to you. You had promised higher and greater things of yourself. There will not be wanting men who are completely worthy and hard-working. Stolid pack-animals are much more fit for carrying loads than thoroughbred horses: who ever subdued their noble speed with a heavy burden? Consider too how much anxiety you have in submitting yourself to such a weight of responsibility: you are dealing with the human belly. A hungry people neither listens to reason nor is mollified by fair treatment or swayed by any appeals. Quite recently, within a few days after Gaius Caesar died – still feeling very upset (if the dead have feelings) because he saw that the Roman people were still surviving, with a supply of food for seven or at most eight days, while he was building bridges with boats and playing with the resources of the empire – we faced the worst of all afflictions, even to those under siege, a shortage of provisions. His imitation of a mad foreign king doomed in his pride, nearly cost the city destruction and famine and the universal collapse that follows famine. What then must those have felt who had charge of the corn supply, when they were threatened with stones, weapons, fire – and Gaius? With a huge pretence they managed to conceal the great evil lurking in the vitals of the state – and assuredly they had good reason. For certain ailments must be treated while the patient is unaware of them: knowing about their disease has caused the death of many.

You must retire to these pursuits which are quieter, safer and more important. Do you think it is the same thing whether you are overseeing the transfer of corn into granaries, unspoilt by the dishonesty and careless-ness of the shippers, and taking care that it does not get damp and then ruined through heat, and that it tallies in measure and weight; or whether you take up these sacred and lofty studies, from which you will learn the substance of god, and his will, his mode of life, his shape; what fate awaits your soul; where nature lays us to rest when released from our bodies; what is the force which supports all the heaviest elements of this world at the centre, suspends the light elements above, carries fire to the highest part, and sets the stars in motion with their proper changes – and learn other things in succession which are full of tremendous marvels? You really should leave the ground and turn your thoughts to these studies. Now while the blood is hot you should make your way with vigour to better things. In this kind of life you will find much that is worth your study: the love and practice of the virtues, forgetfulness of the passions, the know-ledge of how to live and die, and a life of deep tranquillity.

Indeed the state of all who are preoccupied is wretched, but the most wretched are those who are toiling not even at their own preoccupations, but must regulate their sleep by another's, and their walk by another's pace, and obey orders in those freest of all things, loving and hating. If such people want to know how short their lives are, let them reflect how small a portion is their own.

So, when you see a man repeatedly wearing the robe of office, or one whose name is often spoken in the Forum, do not envy him: these things are won at the cost of life. In order that one year may be dated from their names they will waste all their own years. Life has left some men struggling at the start of their careers before they could force their way to the height of their ambition. Some men, after they have crawled through a thousand indignities to the supreme dignity, have been assailed by the gloomy thought that all their labours were but for the sake of an epitaph. Some try to adjust their extreme old age to new hopes as though it were youth, but find its weakness fails them in the midst of efforts that overtax it. It is a shameful sight when an elderly man runs out of breath while he is pleading in court for litigants who are total strangers to him, and trying to win the applause of the ignorant bystanders. It is disgraceful to see a man collapsing in the middle of his duties, worn out more by his life-style than by his labours. Disgraceful too is it when a man dies in the midst of going through his accounts, and his heir, long kept waiting, smiles in relief. I cannot resist telling you of an instance that occurs to me. Sextus Turannius was an old man known to be scrupulous and diligent, who, when he was ninety, at his own request was given retirement from his office by Gaius Caesar. He then ordered himself to be laid out on his bed and lamented by the assembled household as though he were dead. The house bewailed its old master's leisure, and did not cease its mourning until his former job was restored to him. Is it really so pleasant to die in harness? That is the feeling of many people: their desire for their work outlasts their ability to do it. They fight against their own bodily weakness, and they regard old age as a hardship on no other grounds than that it puts them on the shelf. The law does not make a man a soldier after fifty or a senator after sixty: men find it more difficult to gain leisure from themselves than from the law. Meanwhile, as they rob and are robbed, as they disturb each other's peace, as they make each other miserable, their lives pass without satisfaction, without pleasure, without mental improvement. No one keeps death in view, no one refrains from hopes that look far ahead; indeed, some people even arrange things that are beyond life – massive tombs, dedications of public buildings, shows for their funerals, and ostentatious burials. But in truth, such people's funerals should be conducted with torches and wax tapers, as though they had lived the shortest of lives.

Consolation to Helvia

Dearest mother, I have often had the urge to console you and often restrained it. Many things encouraged me to venture to do so. First, I thought I would be laying aside all my troubles when I had at least wiped away your tears, even if I could not stop them coming. Then, I did not doubt that I would have more power to raise you up if I had first risen myself. Moreover, I was afraid that though Fortune was conquered by me she might conquer someone close to me. So, staunching my own cut with my hand I was doing my best to crawl forward to bind up your wounds. There were, on the other hand, considerations which delayed my purpose. I realized that your grief should not be intruded upon while it was fresh and agonizing, in case the consolations themselves should rouse and inflame it: for an illness too nothing is more harmful than premature treatment. So I was waiting until your grief of itself should lose its force and, being softened by time to endure remedies, it would allow itself to be touched and handled. Moreover, although I consulted all the works written by the most famous authors to control and moderate grief, I couldn't find any example of someone who had comforted his own dear ones when he himself was the subject of their grief. So in this unprecedented situation I hesitated, fearing that I would be offering not consolation but further irritation. Consider, too, that a man lifting his head from the very funeral pyre must need some novel vocabulary not drawn from ordinary everyday condolence to comfort his own dear ones. But every great and overpowering grief must take away the capacity to choose words, since it often stifles the voice itself. Anyway, I'll try my best, not trusting in my cleverness, but because being myself the comforter I can thereby be the most effective comfort. As you never refused me anything I hope you will not refuse me this at least (though all grief is stubborn), to be willing that I should set a limit to your desolation.

Consider how much I have promised myself from your indulgence. I don't doubt that I shall have more influence over you than your grief, than which nothing has more influence over the wretched. So in order not to join battle with it at once, I'll first support it and offer it a lot of encouragement: I shall expose and reopen all the wounds which have already healed. Someone will object: 'What kind of consolation is this, to bring back forgotten ills and to set the mind in view of all its sorrows when it can scarcely endure one?' But let him consider that those disorders which are so dangerous that they have gained ground in spite of treatment can generally be treated by opposite methods. Therefore I shall offer to the mind all its sorrows, all its mourning garments: this will not be a gentle prescription for healing, but cautery and the knife. What shall I achieve? That a soul which has conquered so many miseries will be ashamed to worry about one more wound in a body which already has so many scars. So let those people go on weeping and wailing whose self-indulgent minds have been weakened by long prosperity, let them collapse at the threat of the most trivial injuries; but let those who have spent all their years suffering disasters endure the worst afflictions with a brave and resolute staunchness. Everlasting misfortune does have one blessing, that it ends up by toughening those whom it constantly afflicts.

Fortune has given you no respite from the most woeful sorrows, not even excepting the day of your birth. As soon as you were born, no, even while being born, you lost your mother, and on the threshold of life you were in a sense exposed. You grew up under the care of a stepmother, and you actually forced her to become a real mother by showing her all the deference and devotion which can be seen even in a daughter. Yet even having a good stepmother costs every child a good deal. You lost your uncle, kindest, best and bravest of men, when you were awaiting his arrival; and lest Fortune should lessen her cruelty by dividing it, within a month you buried your dearest husband by whom you had three children. This sorrow was announced to you when you were already grieving, and when indeed all your children were away, as if your misfortunes were concentrated on purpose into that time so that your grief would have nowhere to turn for relief. I pass over all the dangers, all the fears you endured as they assailed you unceasingly. But recently into the same lap from which you had let go three grandchildren you received back the bones of three grandchildren. Within twenty days of burying my son, who died as you held and kissed him, you heard that I had been taken away. This only you had lacked – to grieve for the living.

Of all the wounds which have ever pierced your body this last one is, I admit, the worst. It has not simply broken the skin but cut into your breast and vital parts. But just as recruits, even when superficially wounded, cry aloud and dread being handled by doctors more than the sword, while veterans, even if severely wounded, patiently and without a groan allow their wounds to be cleaned as though their bodies did not belong to them; so you must now offer yourself bravely for treatment. Come, put away wailings and lamentations and all the other usual noisy manifestations of feminine grief. For all your sorrows have been wasted on you if you have not yet learned how to be wretched. Do I seem to have dealt boldly with you? I have kept away not one of your misfortunes from you, but piled them all up in front of you.

I have done this courageously for I decided to conquer your grief, not to cheat it. But I shall do this, I think, first of all if I show that I am suffering nothing for which I could be called wretched, let alone make my relations wretched; then if I turn to you and show that your fortune, which is wholly dependent on mine, is also not painful.

First I shall deal with the fact, which your love is longing to hear, that I am suffering no affliction. I shall make it clear, if I can, that those very circumstances which you think are crushing me can be borne; but if you cannot believe that, at least I shall be more pleased with myself for being happy in conditions which normally make men wretched. There is no need to believe others about me: I am telling you firmly that I am not wretched, so that you won't be agitated by uncertainty. To reassure you further, I shall add that I cannot even be made wretched.

We are born under circumstances that would be favourable if we did not abandon them. It was nature's intention that there should be no need of great equipment for a good life: every individual can make himself happy. External goods are of trivial importance and without much influence in either direction: prosperity does not elevate the sage and adversity does not depress him. For he has always made the effort to rely as much as possible on himself and to derive all delight from himself. So what? Am I calling myself a sage? Certainly not. For if I could claim that, not only would I be denying that I was wretched but I would be asserting that I was the most fortunate of all men and coming close to god. As it is, doing what is sufficient to alleviate all wretchedness, I have surrendered myself to wise men, and as I am not yet strong enough to help myself I have gone over to another camp – I mean those who can easily protect themselves and their followers. They have ordered me to take a firm stand, like a sentry on guard, and to foresee all the attacks and all the onslaughts of Fortune long before they hit me. She falls heavily on those to whom she is unexpected; the man who is always expecting her easily withstands her. For an enemy's arrival too scatters those whom it catches off guard; but those who have prepared in advance for the coming conflict, being properly drawn up and equipped, easily withstand the first onslaught, which is the most violent. Never have I trusted Fortune, even when she seemed to offer peace. All those blessings which she kindly bestowed on me – money, public office, influence – I relegated to a place whence she could claim them back without bothering me. I kept a wide gap between them and me, with the result that she has taken them away, not torn them away. No man has been shattered by the blows of Fortune unless he was first deceived by her favours. Those who loved her gifts as if they were their own for ever, who wanted to be admired on account of them, are laid low and grieve when the false and transient pleasures desert their vain and childish minds, ignorant of every stable pleasure. But the man who is not puffed up in good times does not collapse either when they change. His fortitude is already tested and he maintains a mind unconquered in the face of either condition: for in the midst of prosperity he has tried his own strength against adversity. So I have never believed that there was any genuine good in the things which everyone prays for; what is more, I have found them empty and daubed with showy and deceptive colours, with nothing inside to match their appearance. And now in these so-called evils I find nothing so terrible and harsh as the general opinion threatened. Certainly the word 'exile' itself now enters the ears more harshly through a sort of conviction and popular belief, and strikes the listener as something gloomy and detestable. For that is the people's verdict, but wise men on the whole reject the people's decrees.

So, putting aside this judgement of the majority who

are carried away by the surface appearance of things, whatever the grounds for believing in it, let us examine the reality of exile. Clearly a change of place. I must not seem to restrict its force and remove its worst feature, so I agree that this change of place brings with it the disadvantages of poverty, disgrace and contempt. I shall deal with these later; meanwhile I wish first to examine what distress the change of place itself involves.

'It is unbearable to be deprived of your country.' Come now, look at this mass of people whom the buildings of huge Rome can scarcely hold: most of that crowd are deprived of their country. They have flocked together from their towns and colonies, in fact from the whole world, some brought by ambition, some by the obligation of public office, some by the duties of an envoy, some by self-indulgence seeking a place conveniently rich in vice, some by a love of liberal studies, some by the public shows; some have been attracted by friendship, some by their own energy which has found a wide field for displaying its qualities; some have come to sell their beauty, others their eloquence. Absolutely every type of person has hastened into the city which offers high rewards for both virtues and vices. Take a roll-call of all of them and ask each where he comes from: you will see that most of them have left their own homes and come to a very great and beautiful city, but not their own. Then move away from this city, which in a way can be said to belong to all, and go around all the others: in every one a large proportion of the population is immigrant. Pass on from those whose lovely and convenient position attracts large numbers, and review deserted places and rocky islands, Sciathus and Seriphus, Gyara and Cossura: you will find no place of exile where somebody does not linger because he wants to. What could be found so bare and with such a steep drop on every side as this rock? What more barren regarding its resources? What more savage regarding its people? What more rugged regarding its geography? What more intemperate regarding its climate? Yet more foreigners than natives live here. Thus, so far is change of locality itself from being a hardship that even this place has enticed some people from their homeland. I've come across people who say that there is a sort of inborn restlessness in the human spirit and an urge to change one's abode; for man is endowed with a mind which is changeable and unsettled: nowhere at rest, it darts about and directs its thoughts to all places known and unknown, a wanderer which cannot endure repose and delights chiefly in novelty. This will not surprise you if you consider its original source. It was not made from heavy, earthly material, but came down from that heavenly spirit: but heavenly things are by nature always in motion, fleeing and driven on extremely fast. Look at the planets which light up the world: not one is at rest. The sun glides constantly, moving on from place to place, and although it revolves with the universe its motion is nevertheless opposite to that of the firmament itself: it races through all the signs of the zodiac and never stops; its motion is everlasting as it journeys from one point to another. All the planets forever move round and pass by: as the constraining law of nature has ordained they are borne from point of point. When through fixed periods of years they have completed their courses they will start again upon their former circuits. How silly then to imagine that the human mind, which is formed of the same elements as divine beings, objects to movement and change of abode, while the divine nature finds delight and even self-preservation in continual and very rapid change.

Well, now, turn your attention from heavenly to human matters and you will see that whole nations and peoples have changed their abode. What are Greek cities doing in the midst of barbarian territories? Why do we hear the Macedonian language among Indians and Persians? Scythia and all that wide region of fierce and untamed tribes reveal Achaean cities established on the shores of the Pontus. People were not put off from migrating there by the endlessly severe winter or the savage character of the natives which matched their climate. There is a crowd of Athenians in Asia; Miletus has sent out all over the place enough people to colonize seventy-five cities; the whole of the Italian coast which is washed by the lower sea was once Greater Greece. Asia claims the Etruscans as her own; Tyrians live in Africa, Phoenicians in Spain; Greeks penetrated into Gaul and Gauls into Greece; the Pyrenees did not block the passage of the Germans – through trackless, through unknown territory has ventured the restlessness of men, and behind them came their wives and children and parents stricken in years. Some of them, driven about in their long wanderings, did not choose their goal deliberately, but through weariness settled at the nearest place; others by force of arms established their right in a foreign country. Some tribes were drowned while they sought unknown regions; others settled where they were stranded by running out of supplies. They did not all have the same reason for abandoning one homeland for another. Some, escaping the destruction of their cities by enemy attack, were driven to other territory when they lost their own; some were banished by civil strife; others were sent out to relieve the burden of overpopulation; others fled from disease or constant earthquakes or some intolerable deficiencies in their barren soil; others were tempted by the exaggerated report of a fertile shore. Different reasons roused different peoples to leave their homes; but this at least is clear, nothing has stayed where it was born. The human race is always on the move: in so large a world there is every day some change – new cities are founded, and new names of nations are born as former ones disappear or are absorbed into a stronger one. But what else are all these national migrations than banishments of a people? Why should I drag you through the whole cycle? Why bother to mention Antenor who founded Patavium, and Evander who settled the Arcadian kingdom on the banks of the Tiber? What about Diomedes and the others, both conquerors and conquered, who were scattered over alien lands by the Trojan War? Why, the Roman empire itself looks back to an exile as its founder, a man who was driven out when his homeland was captured and, taking a few survivors, was forced by fear of the victor to make a long journey which brought him to Italy. What a number of colonies this people in turn has sent out to every province! – wherever the Romans have conquered they dwell.

People volunteered for this kind of emigration, and even old men leaving their altars followed the settlers overseas. The point does not need any more illustration, but I will just add one which hits you in the eye: this island itself has often changed its inhabitants. To leave aside earlier events which are obscured by antiquity, the Greeks who now live in Massilia after leaving Phocis first settled in this island. It is not clear what drove them from it, whether the harsh climate, or being in sight of the superior power of Italy, or the lack of harbours. For clearly the reason was not the savagery of the inhabitants, since they settled among what were then the fiercest and most uncivilized peoples in Gaul. Subsequently the Ligurians crossed over to the island, and the Spaniards too, as is clear from the similarity of their customs: for the Corsicans wear the same kind of head-covering and shoes as the Cantabrians, and some of their words are the same – only some, for their language as a whole, through association with Greeks and Ligurians, has lost its native elements. Next, two colonies of Roman citizens were brought there, one by Marius and one by Sulla: so often has the population of this barren and thorny rock changed! In a word, you will hardly find a single country still inhabited by its original natives: everywhere the people are of mixed and imported stock. One group has followed another: one longed for what another scorned; one was driven out from where he had expelled others. So fate has decreed that nothing maintains the same condition forever.

To compensate for the actual change of place and forgetting about the other inconveniences attached to exile, Varro, most learned of Romans, considers we have this sufficient remedy, that wherever we come we have the same order of nature to deal with. Marcus Brutus thinks this is enough, that exiles can carry with them their own virtues. Even if anyone thinks that these points taken separately are insufficient to console the exile, he will admit that in combination they carry great weight. For how little have we lost, when the two finest things of all will accompany us wherever we go, universal nature and our individual virtue. Believe me, this was the intention of whoever formed the universe, whether all-powerful god, or incorporeal reason creating mighty works, or divine spirit penetrating all things from greatest to smallest with even pressure, or fate and the unchanging sequence of causation – this, I say, was the intention, that only the most worthless of our possessions should come into the power of another. Whatever is best for a human being lies outside human control: it can be neither given nor taken away. The world you see, nature's greatest and most glorious creation, and the human mind which gazes and wonders at it, and is the most splendid part of it, these are our own everlasting possessions and will remain with us as long as we ourselves remain. So, eager and upright, let us hasten with bold steps wherever circumstances take us, and let us journey through any countries whatever: there can be no place of exile within the world since nothing within the world is alien to men. From whatever point on the earth's surface you look up to heaven the same distance lies between the realms of gods and men. Accordingly, provided my eyes are not withdrawn from that spectacle, of which they never tire;

provided I may look upon the sun and the moon and gaze at the other planets; provided I may trace their risings and settings, their periods and the causes of their travelling faster or slower; provided I may behold all the stars that shine at night – some fixed, others not travelling far afield but circling within the same area; some suddenly shooting forth, and others dazzling the eye with scattered fire, as if they are falling, or gliding past with a long trail of blazing light; provided I can commune with these and, so far as humans may, associate with the divine, and provided I can keep my mind always directed upwards, striving for a vision of kindred things – what does it matter what ground I stand on?

'But this country is not fertile in lush or fruitful trees; no large and navigable rivers irrigate it with their channels; it produces nothing which other nations want, being scarcely fertile enough to support its own inhabitants. No valuable marble is quarried here, no veins of gold and silver are mined.' Petty is the mind which delights in earthly things: it should be led away to those things which appear everywhere equally, everywhere equally lustrous. There is this too to consider, that earthly things stand in the way of genuine goods through a wayward belief in false goods. The longer people extend their colonnades, the higher they build their towers, the wider they stretch their walks, the deeper they dig their summer grottoes, the more massively they raise the roofs of their dining-halls, so much the more will there be to cut off the sight of heaven. Fate has cast you into a land where the most luxurious shelter is a hut. Truly you have a petty spirit which meanly comforts itself, if you put up with this bravely because you know about the hut of Romulus. Say rather 'This humble shack gives shelter, I suppose, to the virtues. Soon it will be more elegant than any temple when justice is seen to be there, and temperance, wisdom, piety, a system for the right allotment of all duties, and the knowledge of man and god. No place is narrow which can hold this assembly of such great virtues; no exile is burdensome when you can have this company with you.'

In his treatise 'On Virtue' Brutus says that he saw Marcellus in exile at Mytilene, living as happily as human nature allows, and never more keen on liberal studies than at that time. And so he adds that when he was about to return without Marcellus, he himself seemed to be going into exile rather than leaving the other in exile. How much more fortunate was Marcellus at that time when he won the favour of Brutus for his exile than when he won the favour of the state for his consulship! What a man that was who caused someone to feel himself an exile because he was leaving an exile behind! What a man he was to have won the admiration of a man whom even his kinsman Cato had to admire! Brutus also says that Gaius Caesar had sailed past Mytilene because he could not bear the sight of a great man in disgrace. Indeed, the senate obtained his recall by public petition: they were so anxious and sorrowful that they all seemed to share Brutus' feelings on that day, and to be pleading not for Marcellus but for themselves, in case they would be exiled if deprived of him. But he achieved much more on that day when Brutus could not bear to leave, nor Caesar to see, him in exile. For both gave him testimony: Brutus grieved to return without Marcellus, and Caesar blushed. Can you doubt that Marcellus, being the great man he was, often encouraged himself thus to endure his exile with equanimity? 'Being without your country is not misery: you have thoroughly taught yourself by your studies to know that to a wise man every place is his country. Besides, was not the man who caused your exile himself absent from his country for ten consecutive years? No doubt the reason was to enlarge his domains – yet he certainly was absent. See, now he is summoned to Africa which is full of threats of further war; to Spain which is reviving its forces shattered by defeat; to treacherous Egypt – in short to the whole world which is watchful for an opportunity against the stricken empire. Which problem shall he face first? To which quarter take his stand? His own victorious course will drive him throughout the world. Let the nations honour and worship him; live yourself content with Brutus as your admirer.'

Well did Marcellus, then, endure his exile, nor did his change of abode cause any change at all in his mind though poverty attended it. But there is no evil in poverty, as anyone knows who has not yet arrived at the lunatic state of greed and luxury, which ruin everything. For how little is needed to support a man! And who can lack this if he has any virtue at all? As far as I am concerned, I know that I have lost not wealth but distractions. The body's needs are few: it wants to be free from cold, to banish hunger and thirst with nourishment; if we long for anything more we are exerting ourselves to serve our vices, not our needs. We do not need to scour every ocean, or to load our bellies with the slaughter of animals, or to pluck shellfish from the unknown shores of the furthest sea. May gods and goddesses destroy those whose luxury passes the bounds of an empire that already awakens envy. They seek to stock their pretentious kitchens by hunting beyond the Phasis, and they aren't ashamed to ask for birds from the Parthians, from whom we have not yet exacted vengeance. From all sides they collect everything familiar to a fastidious glutton. From the furthest sea is brought food which their stomachs, weakened by a voluptuous diet, can scarcely receive. They vomit in order to eat, and eat in order to vomit, and banquets for which they ransack the whole world they do not even deign to digest. If someone despises all that, what harm can poverty do him? If he longs for it, poverty even does him good: for against his will he is being cured, and if even under compulsion he does not take his medicine, for a time at least his inability to have those things looks like unwillingness. Gaius Caesar, whom I think nature produced as an example of the effect of supreme wickedness in a supreme position, dined in one day at a cost of ten million sesterces; and though helped in this by everyone's ingenuity he could scarcely discover how to spend the tribute from three provinces on one dinner. Poor wretches, whose appetite is only tempted by expensive foods! Yet it is not an exquisite taste or some delightful effect on the palate that makes them expensive, but their scarcity and the difficulty of procuring them. Otherwise, if these people would agree to return to good sense, where is the need for all these skills that serve the belly? What need for importing, or laying waste the woodlands, or ransacking the ocean? All around food lies ready which nature has distributed in every place; but men pass it by as though blind to it, and they scour every country, they cross the seas, and they whet their appetite at great expense when at little cost they could satisfy it. I want to say to them: 'Why do you launch your ships? Why do you arm your bands against both beasts and men? Why do you tear around in such a panic? Why do you pile wealth upon wealth? You really must consider how small your bodies are. Is it not madness and the worst form of derangement to want so much though you can hold so little? Therefore, though you may increase your income and extend your estates, you will never increase the capacity of your bodies. Though your business may do well and warfare bring you profit, though you hunt down and gather your food from every side, you will not have anywhere to store your supplies. Why do you seek out so many things? To be sure, our ancestors were unhappy, whose virtue even now props up our vices, who procured their food with their own hands, who slept on the ground, whose dwellings did not yet glitter with gold nor their temples with precious stones – and so in those days they swore solemn oaths by gods of clay and, having invoked them, returned to the enemy to certain death rather than break their word. To be sure, our dictator who gave audience to the Samnite envoys while with his own hand he cooked the simplest sort of food (the hand which already had frequently smitten the enemy and placed a laurel wreath on the lap of Capitoline Jupiter) – he lived less happily than Apicius in our time, who in the city from

which philosophers were once banished as corrupters of
the youth, polluted the age by his teaching as professor
of cookery.' It is worth hearing what happened to him.
When he had spent a hundred million sesterces in his
kitchen, when he had drunk up at every one of his
carousals all those imperial gifts and the enormous rev-
enue of the Capitol, then for the first time he was forced
by the weight of his debts to look into his accounts. He
reckoned he would have ten million sesterces left, and
that living on ten million would be starvation: so he
poisoned himself. What luxury, if ten million meant
poverty! How then can you think that it is the amount
of money that matters and not the attitude of mind?
Someone dreaded having ten million, and what others
pray for he escaped by poison. But indeed for a man of
such perverted mentality that last drink was the best
thing for him. It was when he was not merely enjoying
but boasting of his huge banquets, when he was making
a display of his vices, when he was drawing public
attention to his vulgar displays, when he was tempting
young people to imitate him (who even without bad
examples are naturally impressionable) – then it was that
he was really eating and drinking poisons. Such is the
fate of those who measure wealth not by the standard
of reason, whose limits are fixed, but by that of a vicious
life-style governed by boundless, uncontrollable caprice.
Nothing satisfies greed, but even a little satisfies nature.
So an exile's poverty brings no hardship; for no place of
exile is so barren that it cannot abundantly support a man.

'But,' says someone, 'the exile is going to miss his
clothes and home.' These too he will miss only as far as

he needs them – and he will lack neither house nor covering; for the body needs as little for protection as for food. Nature has not made any of man's essentials laborious as well. But he must have richly dyed purple clothes, woven with gold thread and decorated with multicoloured patterns: it is his fault, not nature's, if he feels poor. Even if you give him back all he has lost, you'll be wasting your time; for once he is back from exile he will feel a greater lack compared with his desires than he felt as an exile compared with his former possessions. But he must have furniture gleaming with gold vessels and antique silver plate wrought by famous artists, bronze made valuable because a few lunatics want it, a crowd of slaves which would throng a house however large, beasts of burden with bodies bloated with force-feeding, marbles from every land: though he piles all these up, they will never sate his insatiable soul; just as no amount of fluid will satisfy one whose craving arises not from lack of water but from burning internal fever: for that is not a thirst but a disease. Nor is this true only of money or food: the same feature is found in every desire which arises not from a lack but from a vice. However much you heap up for it will not mark the end of greed, only a stage in it. So the man who restrains himself within the bounds set by nature will not notice poverty; the man who exceeds these bounds will be pursued by poverty however rich he is. Life's necessities are found even in places of exile, superfluities not even in kingdoms. It is the mind that creates our wealth, and this goes with us into exile, and in the harshest desert places it finds sufficient to nourish the body and revels in the enjoyment of its own goods. Money in no way concerns the mind any more than it concerns the gods. All those things which are revered by minds untaught and enslaved to their bodies – marble, gold, silver, great round polished tables – are earthly burdens which a soul pure and conscious of its nature cannot love: for it is light and unencumbered, and destined to soar aloft whenever it is released from the body. Meanwhile, so far as it is not hampered by our limbs and this heavy burden that envelops us, it surveys things divine with swift and winged thought. So the soul can never suffer exile, being free and akin to the gods and equal to all the universe and all time. For its thought encompasses the whole of heaven, and journeys into all past and future time. This wretched body, the chain and prison of the soul, is tossed hither and thither; upon it punishment and pillage and disease wreak havoc: but the soul itself is holy and eternal, and it cannot be assailed with violence.

In case you think I am simply using the teaching of philosophers to make light of the trials of poverty, which no one feels to be a burden unless he thinks it that, first consider that by far the greater proportion of men are poor, but you will not see them looking at all more gloomy and anxious than the rich. In fact, I rather suspect that they are happier in proportion as their minds have less to harry them. Let us pass on to the rich: how frequently are they just like the poor! When they travel abroad their luggage is restricted, and whenever they are forced to hasten their journey they dismiss their retinue of attendants. When they are serving in the army, how little of their belongings do they keep with them, since camp discipline forbids any luxury! Nor is it only special conditions of time and place which put them on a level with the poor in their needs: when on occasion they get tired of their riches they choose certain days on which they dine on the ground and, putting aside their gold and silver vessels, use earthenware ones. What lunatics, to covet sometimes a condition they always dread! What mental darkness, what ignorance of the truth blinds those who, though afflicted by the fear of poverty, yet take pleasure in imitating it! For my part, whenever I look back at the fine examples of antiquity, I am ashamed to find consolations for poverty, since the luxury of the times has reached the point where an exile's allowance is more than the inheritance of leading men of old. We all know that Homer had one slave, Plato had three, and Zeno, the founder of the strict and manly Stoic philosophy, had none. Will anyone on that account say that they lived wretchedly without himself seeming to all by his words to be utterly wretched? Menenius Agrippa, who kept the public peace by acting as mediator between patricians and plebeians, was buried by public subscription. Atilius Regulus, while he was routing the Carthaginians in Africa, wrote to tell the senate that his hired worker had gone off and abandoned his farm: the senate voted that during Regulus' absence the farm should be managed by the state. Was it not worth being without a slave so that the Roman people might become his tenant? Scipio's daughters received a dowry from the state treasury because their father had left them nothing: assuredly it was right for the Roman people to offer tribute to Scipio once, since he was always exacting it from Carthage. Happy were the girls' husbands whose father-in-law was the Roman people! Do you think those whose pantomime actresses marry with a dowry of a million sesterces are happier than Scipio, whose children had the senate for their guardian and received solid copper money as a dowry? Could anyone despise poverty with a pedigree so distinguished? Could an exile resent lacking anything, when Scipio lacked a dowry, Regulus a hired worker, Menenius a funeral: when for all of them supplying their need was all the more honourable simply because they had the need? And so, with these men pleading her cause poverty wins not only acquittal but high esteem.

One might reply, 'Why do you make an artificial separation of those things which can be borne separately but not in combination? You can put up with a change of place if only the place is changed. You can put up with poverty if there is no disgrace, which even alone usually crushes the spirit.' In answer to this man who aims to frighten me by an accumulation of ills, this must be said: 'If you have the strength to tackle any one aspect of misfortune you can tackle all. When once virtue has toughened the mind it renders it invulnerable on every side. If greed, the most overmastering plague of the human race, has relaxed its grip, ambition will not stand in your way. If you regard your last day not as a punishment but as a law of nature, the breast from which you have banished the dread of death no fear will dare to enter. If you consider that sexual desire was given to man not for enjoyment but for the propagation of the race, once you are free of this violent and destructive passion rooted in your vitals, every other desire will leave you undisturbed. Reason routs the vices not one by one but all together: the victory is final and complete.' Do you think that any wise man can be affected by disgrace, one who relies entirely on himself and holds aloof from common beliefs? A disgraceful death is worse than disgrace: yet Socrates went to prison with the same expression he wore when he once snubbed the Thirty Tyrants – and his presence robbed even prison of disgrace, for where Socrates was could not seem a prison. Who is so blind to the truth that he thinks it was a disgrace to Marcus Cato that he was twice defeated in his bid for the praetorship and consulship? The disgrace belonged to the praetorship and consulship which were being honoured by Cato. No man is despised by another unless he is first despised by himself. An abject and debased mind is susceptible to such insult; but if a man stirs himself to face the worst of disasters and defeats the evils which overwhelm others, then he wears those very sorrows like a sacred badge. For we are naturally disposed to admire more than anything else the man who shows fortitude in adversity. When Aristides was being led to execution at Athens, everyone who met him cast down his eyes and groaned, as though it was not merely a just man but Justice herself who was being punished. Yet one man actually spat in his face. He could have resented this because he knew that only a foul-mouthed man would dare to do it. Instead he wiped his face, and with a smile he said to the magistrate escorting him: 'Warn that fellow not to give such a vulgar yawn another time.' This was to retaliate insult upon insult. I know some people say that nothing is worse than scorn and that even death seems preferable. To these I shall reply that exile too is often free from any kind of scorn. If a great man falls and remains great as he lies, people no more despise him than they stamp on a fallen temple, which the devout still worship as much as when it was standing.

Dearest mother, since you have no cause on my account to drive you to endless tears it follows that reasons regarding yourself are urging you to weep. Well, there are two: you are bothered either because you seem to have lost some protection, or because you cannot endure the very thought of doing without me.

The first point I must touch upon only slightly, for I know that your heart loves your dear ones for themselves alone. Let those mothers reflect on this who exploit their children's influence with a woman's lack of influence; who, because women cannot hold office, seek power through their sons; who both drain their sons' inheritances and try to get them; who exhaust their sons by lending their eloquence to others. Whereas you have taken the greatest pleasure in your sons' gifts and made the least use of them; you have always set a limit to our generosity without limiting your own; while your father was still alive you actually gave gifts to your wealthy sons; you administered our inheritances as though you were earnestly looking after your own and being scrupulously provident with another's; you were cautious in using our influence, as if it were someone else's, and in our spells in office you had no part except your pleasure and the expenses. Your love never had regard for self-interest: therefore, now that your son has been taken from you, you cannot feel the lack of those things which you never thought concerned you when he was safe and sound.

I must direct my consolation entirely to that point from which arises the true force of a mother's grief. You say, 'So I am deprived of my dearest son's embrace; I can't enjoy seeing him or talking to him. Where is he whose appearance smoothed my troubled brow, to whom I confided all my woes? Where are our conversations of which I never tired? Where are his studies which I shared with more than a feminine eagerness and more than a mother's intimacy? Where are our meetings? Where is the unfailing boyish glee at the sight of his mother?' To all this you add the actual places where we rejoiced together and socialized, and the reminders of our recent life together which are inevitably the most acute source of mental anguish. For Fortune plotted even this cruel blow against you, that only two days before I was struck down she contrived that you should depart tranquil in mind and fearing no such disaster. It was well that we had lived far apart, and that an absence of some years had prepared you for this blow. By returning you did not gain the pleasure of your son's presence, but you lost the habit of bearing his absence. If you had been away long before you would have borne the loss more bravely, as the very distance between us would have softened the longing. If you had not gone away you would at least have had the final pleasure of seeing your son for two days longer. As it was, cruel fate so arranged it that you could neither be present at my misfortune nor get used to my absence. But the harsher these circumstances are, the greater the courage you must summon up and the more fiercely you must fight, as with an enemy you know and have often defeated. Your blood has not now flowed from an undamaged body: you have been struck exactly where the old scars are.

You must not excuse yourself as being a woman, who has been virtually given the right to indulge excessively, but not endlessly, in tears. With this in view our ancestors allowed widows to mourn their husbands for ten months, in order to compromise by public decree with the stubbornness of female grief. They did not prohibit mourning but they limited it. For to be afflicted with endless sorrow at the loss of someone very dear is foolish self-indulgence, and to feel none is inhuman callousness. The best compromise between love and good sense is both to feel longing and to conquer it. You must not pay regard to certain women whose grief, once assumed, was ended only by death – you know some who never removed the mourning dress they put on when they lost their sons. Your life was braver from its start and expects more from you: the excuse of being a woman does not apply to one from whom all womanly faults have been absent. That worst evil of our time, unchastity, has not numbered you among the majority of women; neither jewels nor pearls have influenced you; the glitter of wealth has not struck you as the greatest blessing of the human race; you were brought up in a strict, old-fashioned home and never deviated into the imitation of worse women which is dangerous even to good ones;

you were never ashamed of your fertility as if it taunted you with your advancing years; never did you follow other women who seek only to impress by their looks, and hide your pregnancy as if it were an indecent burden, nor did you destroy the hopes of giving birth by abortion; you did not spoil your complexion by paints and cosmetics; you never liked the sort of garment which revealed no more when it was taken off; in you has been seen that matchless ornament, that loveliest beauty which is not dependent on any time of life, that greatest glory of all – modesty. So you cannot, in order to justify your grief, claim the name of woman from which your virtues have set you apart: you ought to be as immune to female tears as to female vices. Not even women will allow you to waste away from your wound, but they will tell you to get your necessary mourning speedily over with and rise again comforted, by willing yourself to keep in mind those women whose conspicuous courage has ranked them with great men. Fortune reduced Cornelia's twelve children to two: if you wanted to count Cornelia's bereavements, she had lost ten; if you wanted to appraise them, she had lost the Gracchi. But when those around her were weeping and cursing her fate she forbad them to accuse Fortune, which had given her the Gracchi as her sons. It was a fitting son of this mother who said in the assembly, 'Would you insult the mother who gave me birth?' Yet his mother's words seem to me much more spirited: the son was proud of the parentage of the Gracchi, the mother of their deaths as well. Rutilia followed her son Cotta into exile, and was so single-minded in her devotion that she preferred exile to missing him, and returned home only when he did. And when, restored to favour and a distinguished public figure, he died, she bore his loss as bravely as she had shared his exile, nor was she ever seen to weep after his funeral. She showed courage when he was exiled and wisdom when he died; for nothing stopped her showing her love and nothing induced her to persist in useless and unavailing grief. It is with women like these that I want you to be numbered. You always imitated their way of life, and you will best follow their example in controlling and conquering your sorrow.

I know that this is not something which is in our power and that no strong feeling is under our control, least of all that which arises from sorrow: for it is violent and violently resists every remedy. Sometimes we want to crush it and swallow down our groans, but through the pretended composure of our features the tears pour down. Sometimes we divert our mind with public shows or gladiatorial contests, but in the very midst of the distractions of the spectacles it is undermined by some little reminder of its loss. Therefore it is better to conquer our grief than to deceive it. For if it has withdrawn, being merely beguiled by pleasures and preoccupations, it starts up again and from its very respite gains force to savage us. But the grief that has been conquered by reason is calmed for ever. I am not therefore going to prescribe for you those remedies which I know many people have used, that you divert or cheer yourself by a long or pleasant journey abroad, or spend a lot of time carefully going through your accounts and administering your estate, or constantly be involved in some new activity. All those things help only for a short time; they do not cure grief but hinder it. But I would rather end it than distract it. And so I am leading you to that resource which must be the refuge of all who are flying from Fortune, liberal studies. They will heal your wound, they will withdraw all your melancholy. Even if you had never been familiar with them you would have need of them now. But, so far as the old-fashioned strictness of my father allowed, you have had some acquaintance with the liberal arts, even if you have not mastered them. If only my father, best of men, had been less devoted to ancestral tradition, and had been willing that you be steeped in the teaching of philosophy and not just gain a smattering of it: you would not now have to acquire your defence against Fortune but just bring it forth. He was less inclined to let you pursue your studies because of those women who use books not to acquire wisdom but as the furniture of luxury. Yet thanks to your vigorously inquiring mind you absorbed a lot considering the time you had available: the foundations of all formal studies have been laid. Return now to these studies and they will keep you safe. They will comfort you, they will delight you; and if they genuinely penetrate your mind, never again will grief enter there, or anxiety, or the distress caused by futile and pointless suffering. Your heart will have room for none of these, for to all other failings it has long been closed. Those studies are your most dependable protection, and they alone can snatch you from Fortune's grip.

But until you arrive at this haven which philosophy holds out to you, you must have supports to lean on: so

I want meanwhile to point out your own consolations. Consider my brothers: while they live you have no reason to complain of your fortune. In both you have contrasting virtues to cheer you up: the one achieved public office by his energy, the other in his wisdom despised it. Take comfort in the distinction of the one, the retirement of the other, and the devotion of both. I know the innermost feelings of my brothers. The one fosters his distinction really in order to bring honour to you, while the other has retired into peace and tranquillity in order to have leisure for you. Fortune has done you a service in arranging that your children should bring you both assistance and delight: you can be protected by the distinction of the one and you can enjoy the leisure of the other. They will be rivals in their services to you, and the devotion of two will fill the blank space left by one. I promise you with complete confidence that you will miss nothing but the number of sons.

After these consider too your grandchildren: Marcus, a most charming child – you could not remain sorrowful while looking at him, and no one's heart could suffer anguish too great or too recent not to be soothed by his embrace. Whose tears would his merriment not allay? Whose heart gripped by anxious care would not relax at his lively chatter? Who will not smile at his playfulness? Whose attention, however fixed on his own thoughts, will not be attracted and held by that prattling which no one could tire of? I pray to the gods that he may survive us! May all the cruelty of fate wear itself out and stop at me. Whatever you were destined to suffer as a mother and as a grandmother may I represent. Let the rest of my family flourish undisturbed. I shall not complain of my childlessness or my exile, if only I prove to be the scapegoat for a family that will suffer no more. Embrace Novatilla, who will soon give you great-grandchildren; I had so attached her to myself and adopted her that in losing me she could seem an orphan, though her father is alive. Cherish her for me too. Fortune recently took away her mother, but your love will mean that she will only grieve over her mother's loss but not suffer for it. Now you must shape and compose her character: teaching sinks more deeply into those of impressionable years. Let her grow used to your conversation and be moulded as you think right; you will be giving her a great deal even if you give her only your example. Such a sacred duty as this will act as a cure for you, for only philosophy or honourable occupation can divert from its anguish a heart whose grief springs from love.

I would reckon your father too among your great comforts if he were not absent. As it is, you must now judge his love for you by your love for him, and you will realize how much more just it is for you to preserve yourself for him than sacrifice yourself for me. Whenever excessive grief attacks you and urges you to give way to it, think of your father. Certainly, by giving him so many grandchildren and great-grandchildren you ceased to be his only offspring; but for him the completion of a happy life depends on you. While he lives it is wrong for you to complain that you have lived.

Up to now I have said nothing about your greatest comfort, your sister, that heart most faithful to you into which are poured unreservedly all your anxieties, that soul which has been a mother to us all. You mingled your tears with hers; on her bosom you first began to breathe again. Always indeed she shares your feelings, but in my case she grieves not only for you. She carried me in her arms to Rome. During my long illness it was her loving and motherly nursing that brought me round. When I was a candidate for the quaestorship she supported me and, though she normally lacked the confidence even for conversation or a loud greeting, for my sake love conquered shyness. Neither her sheltered manner of living, nor her modesty (old-fashioned when compared with the prevalent brazenness of women), nor her tranquillity, nor her reserved nature which wanted peace and quiet – none of these prevented her from actually becoming ambitious on my behalf. She, dearest mother, is the source of comfort from which you can revive yourself: cling to her as much as you can in the closest embraces. Sorrowers tend to avoid what they are most fond of and try to give vent to their grief; but you must share all your thoughts with her. Whether you wish to keep this mood or lay it aside, you will find in her either the end of your sorrow or one who will share it. But if I know the wisdom of this paragon of women, she will not allow you to be consumed in profitless anguish, and she will tell you of an edifying episode in her life which I also witnessed.

While actually on a sea voyage she lost her beloved husband, my uncle, whom she had married as a maiden; yet she bore simultaneously the burdens of grief and fear and, though shipwrecked, she rode out the storms and brought his body safely ashore. O how many noble deeds of women are lost in obscurity! If she had chanced to live in the days of old when people frankly admired heroism, how men of genius would have competed to sing the praises of a wife who ignored her physical weakness, ignored the sea which even the bravest must fear, and risked her life to give her husband burial; and while her thoughts were on his funeral had no fears about her own! All the poets have given renown to the woman who offered to die in place of her husband. But this is nobler, to risk one's life to bury one's husband: for that love is greater which wins less through equal danger.

After this it can surprise no one that during the sixteen years her husband governed Egypt she was never seen in public, she received no provincial into her home, she never petitioned her husband for a favour, and she never allowed herself to be petitioned. The result was that a province given to gossip and clever at insulting its rulers, where even those who had avoided wrongdoing did not escape scandal, respected her as a singular pattern of integrity, restrained all licence in its speech (a very difficult achievement where even dangerous witticisms are popular), and even to this day keeps hoping, though it never expects, to see another like her. It would have been a great achievement if she had won the approval of the province for sixteen years; it was even better not to have been noticed there. I do not recall these things in order to list her good qualities (to rehearse them so sketchily is to be unfair to them), but to give you an idea of the high-mindedness of the woman who was not conquered by ambition or greed, those inevitable companions and curses of power; who, facing shipwreck on a disabled boat, was not deterred by the fear of death from clinging to her dead husband and seeking not the means of her own escape but the means of getting his body off for burial. This is the sort of courage you must match, by withdrawing your mind from grief and resolving that no one shall think you regret having had children.

However, whatever you do, inevitably your thoughts will turn to me constantly, and none of your other children will come to your mind more often, not because they are less dear to you but because it is natural to touch more often the part that hurts. So this is how you must think of me – happy and cheerful as if in the best of circumstances. For they are best, since my mind, without any preoccupation, is free for its own tasks, now delighting in more trivial studies, now in its eagerness for the truth rising up to ponder its own nature and that of the universe. It seeks to know first about lands and their location, then the nature of the encompassing sea and its tidal ebb and flow. Then it studies all the awesome expanse which lies between heaven and earth – this nearer space turbulent with thunder, lightning, gales of wind, and falling rain, snow and hail. Finally, having scoured the lower areas it bursts through to the heights and enjoys the noblest sight of divine things and, mindful of its own immortality, it ranges over all that has been and will be throughout all ages.

On Tranquillity of Mind

SERENUS:* When I looked into myself, Seneca, some of
my vices appeared clearly on the surface, so that I could
lay my hand on them; some were more hidden away
in the depths; some were not there all the time but
return at intervals. These last I would say are the most
troublesome: they are like prowling enemies who
pounce on you when occasion offers, and allow you
neither to be at the ready as in war nor at ease as in
peace. However, the state I most find myself in (for why
should I not admit the truth to you as to a doctor?) is
that I am not really free of the vices which I feared and
hated, though not, on the other hand, subject to them:
this puts me in a condition which is not the worst, but
an extremely peevish and quarrelsome one – I am neither
ill nor well. There is no need for you to say that all
virtues are fragile to start with and acquire firmness and
strength with time. I know too that those which toil to
make a good impression, seeking high rank, for example,
and a reputation for eloquence, and whatever depends
on the approval of others, take time to mature – both
those which offer real strength and those which are
tricked out in some sort of dye aimed at popularity have
to wait years until the passage of time gradually produces

* A friend of Seneca's.

their colour. But I'm afraid that habit, which induces firmness in things, may drive this fault more deeply into me: long association brings love of evil as well as good.

I cannot show all at once so much as bit by bit the nature of this mental weakness, which wavers between two choices and does not incline strongly either to right or to wrong: I'll tell you what happens to me and you can find a name for the malady. I have a tremendous love of frugality, I must admit. I don't like a couch decked out ostentatiously; or clothes brought out from a chest or given a sheen by the forceful pressure of weights and a thousand mangles, but homely and inexpensive, and not hoarded to be donned with fuss and bother. I like food which is not prepared and watched over by the household slaves, not ordered many days in advance nor served by a multitude of hands, but readily obtainable and easy to deal with, nothing in it out of the way or expensive, available everywhere, not heavy on the purse or the body, and not destined to come back by the same way it entered. I want my servant to be an ordinary, unskilled, home-born slave; my silver to be the heavy ware of my rustic father without any hallmark; and my table to be without flashy variegated markings and not familiar to the whole town through its many changes of fashionable owners, but set up to be used and not to distract any guest's eyes with pleasure or kindle them with envy. But when I have set up these standards I find my mind dazzled by the fine trappings of some training-school for servants, with the slaves more care-fully clothed and decked with gold than if they were in a public parade, and a whole army of glittering flunkies;

by a house where you even walk on precious stones, where wealth is scattered in every corner, where the roof itself glitters, and the whole populace deferentially attends the ruin of a family heritage. Need I mention pools clear to their depths which flow around the dinner guests, or banquets worthy of their surroundings? After being long given up to frugality I have found myself surrounded by the lavish splendour of luxury echoing all about me. My vision wavers somewhat, for I can raise my mind to face it more easily than my eyes. And so I come back not a worse but a sadder man; I don't move with my head so high among my trivial possessions; and a secret gnawing doubt undermines me whether that life is superior. None of these things is changing me, but none of them fails to shake me.

I decide to follow my teacher's precepts and busy myself in state affairs; I decide to achieve public office – not, of course, because of the purple robe and the lictors' rods, but so that I can be more ready with help for my friends and relations, for all my fellow-citizens, and then for all mankind. Enthusiastically I follow Zeno, Cleanthes, Chrysippus, of whom, by the way, none entered public life and all urged others to do so. But when something has assailed my mind, which is not used to being battered; when something has happened which either is unworthy of me (a common experience in every human life) or cannot easily be dealt with; when unimportant things become time-consuming; I take refuge in leisure and, just like weary flocks of animals, I make my way more quickly home. I decide to restrict my life within its walls, saying, 'Let no one rob me of a single day who is not going to make me an adequate return for such a loss. Let my mind be fixed on itself, cultivate itself, have no external interest – nothing that seeks the approval of another; let it cherish the tranquillity that has no part in public or private concerns.' But when my mind is excited by reading a convincing account of something and spurred on by noble examples, I long to rush into the forum, to speak on behalf of one man and offer help to another, which will at least be an attempt to assist even if it does not succeed, or to curb the pride of someone else grown arrogant by success.

In my studies I suppose it must indeed be better to keep my theme firmly in view and speak to this, while allowing the theme to suggest my words and so dictate the course of an unstudied style of speech. 'Where is the need,' I ask, 'to compose something to last for ages? Why not stop trying to prevent posterity being silent about you? You were born to die, and a silent funeral is less bothersome. So if you must fill your time, write something in a simple style for your own use and not for publication: less toil is needed if you study only for the day.' Again, when my mind is lifted up by the greatness of its thoughts, it becomes ambitious for words and longs to match its higher inspiration with its language, and so produces a style that conforms to the impressiveness of the subject matter. Then it is that I forget my rule and principle of restraint, and I am carried too far aloft by a voice no longer my own.

To cut the matter short, this weakness in my good intentions pursues me in every sphere. I fear that I am gradually getting worse, or (which is more worrying) that I am hanging on an edge like someone always on the point of falling, and that perhaps there is more wrong than I myself can see: for we take too intimate a view of our own characteristics and bias always affects our judgement. I imagine many people could have achieved wisdom if they had not imagined they had already achieved it, if they had not dissembled about some of their own characteristics and turned a blind eye to others. For you have no reason to suppose that we come to grief more through the flattery of others than through our own. Who has dared to tell himself the truth? Who even when surrounded by crowds of toadying sycophants is not his own greatest flatterer? So, I am appealing to you, if you have any cure for this vacillation of mind, to consider me worthy of owing tranquillity to you. I realize that these mental agitations of mine are not dangerous and won't produce a storm. To express my complaint for you in a realistic metaphor, I am harried not by a tempest but by sea-sickness. Whatever my ailment, then, root it out and come to the help of one who is struggling in sight of land.

SENECA: Indeed, Serenus, I have long been silently asking myself to what I should compare such a mental state, and I could find no closer analogy than the condition of those people who have got over a long and serious illness, but are still sometimes mildly affected by onsets of fever and pain, and even when free of the last symptoms are still worried and upset; and, though quite better, offer their hands to doctors and needlessly complain if they feel at all hot. With these people, Serenus, it is not that their bodies are insufficiently healed but that they are insufficiently used to health, just as even a calm sea will show some ripples, especially when it has subsided following a storm. So what you need is not those more radical remedies which we have now finished with – blocking yourself here, being angry with yourself there, threatening yourself sternly somewhere else – but the final treatment, confidence in yourself and the belief that you are on the right path, and not led astray by the many tracks which cross yours of people who are hopelessly lost, though some are wandering not far from the true path. But what you are longing for is great and supreme and nearly divine – not to be shaken. The Greeks call this steady firmness of mind 'euthymia' (Democritus wrote a good treatise about it), but I call it tranquillity, as there is no need to imitate and reproduce the form of Greek words: the point at issue must be indicated by some term which should have the sense but not the form of the Greek name. We are, therefore, seeking how the mind can follow a smooth and steady course, well disposed to itself, happily regarding its own condition and with no interruption to this pleasure, but remaining in a state of peace with no ups and downs: that will be tranquillity. Let us consider in general how this can be achieved: you will then extract what you like from the communal remedy. Meanwhile the whole failing must be dragged out into the open, where everyone will recognize his own share in it. At the same time you will realize how much less trouble you have with your self-revulsion than those people who, tied to some specious declaration and labouring under an impressive title, are stuck with their own pretence more by shame than by desire.

They are all in the same category, both those who are afflicted with fickleness, boredom and a ceaseless change of purpose, and who always yearn for what they have left behind, and those who just yawn from apathy. There are those too who toss around like insomniacs, and keep changing their position until they find rest through sheer weariness. They keep altering the condition of their lives, and eventually stick to that one in which they are trapped not by weariness with further change but by old age which is too sluggish for novelty. There are those too who suffer not from moral steadfastness but from inertia, and so lack the fickleness to live as they wish, and just live as they have begun. In fact there are innumerable characteristics of the malady, but one effect – dissatisfaction with oneself. This arises from mental instability and from fearful and unfulfilled desires, when men do not dare or do not achieve all they long for, and all they grasp at is hope: they are always unbalanced and fickle, an inevitable consequence of living in suspense. They struggle to gain their prayers by every path, and they teach and force themselves to do dishonourable and difficult things; and when their efforts are unrewarded the fruitless disgrace tortures them, and they regret not the wickedness but the frustration of their desires. Then they are gripped by repentance for their attempt and fear of trying again, and they are undermined by the restlessness of a mind that can discover no outlet, because they can neither control nor obey their desires, by the dithering of a life that cannot see its way ahead, and by the lethargy of a soul stagnating amid its abandoned hopes. All these afflictions are worse when, through hatred of their toilsome failure, men have retreated into idleness and private studies which are unbearable to a mind aspiring to public service, keen on activity, and restless by nature because of course it is short of inner resources. In consequence, when the pleasures have been removed which busy people derive from their actual activities, the mind cannot endure the house, the solitude, the walls, and hates to observe its own isolation. From this arises that boredom and self-dissatisfaction, that turmoil of a restless mind and gloomy and grudging endurance of our leisure, especially when we are ashamed to admit the reasons for it and our sense of shame drives the agony inward, and our desires are trapped in narrow bounds without escape and stifle themselves. From this arise melancholy and mourning and a thousand vacillations of a wavering mind, buoyed up by the birth of hope and sickened by the death of it. From this arises the state of mind of those who loathe their own leisure and complain that they have nothing to do, and the bitterest envy at the promotion of others. For unproductive idleness nurtures malice, and because they themselves could not prosper they want everyone else to be ruined. Then from this dislike of others' success and despair of their own, their minds become enraged against fortune, complain about the times, retreat into obscurity, and brood over their own sufferings until they become sick and tired of themselves. For the human mind is naturally mobile and enjoys activity. Every chance of stimulation and distraction is welcome to it – even more welcome to all those inferior characters who actually enjoy being worn out by busy activity. There are certain bodily sores which welcome the hands that will hurt them, and long to be touched, and a foul itch loves to be scratched: in the same way I would say that those minds on which desires have broken out like horrid sores take delight in toil and aggravation. For some things delight our bodies even when they cause some pain, like turning over to change a side that is not yet tired and repeatedly shifting to keep cool: so Achilles in Homer lay now on his face, now on his back, trying to settle in different positions, and like an invalid could endure nothing for long but used his restlessness as a cure. Hence men travel far and wide, wandering along foreign shores and making trial by land and sea of their restlessness, which always hates what is around it. 'Let's now go to Campania.' Then when they get bored with luxury – 'Let's visit uncultivated areas; let's explore the woodlands of Bruttium and Lucania.' And yet amid the wilds some delight is missing by which their pampered eyes can find relief from the tedious squalor of these unsightly regions. 'Let's go to Tarentum, with its cele-brated harbour and mild winters, an area prosperous enough for a large population even in antiquity.' 'Let's now make our way to the city' – too long have their ears missed the din of applause: now they long to enjoy even the sight of human blood. They make one journey after another and change spectacle for spectacle. As Lucretius says, 'Thus each man ever flees himself.' But to what end, if he does not escape himself? He pursues and dogs himself as his own most tedious companion. And so we must realize that our difficulty is not the fault of the places but of ourselves. We are weak in enduring anything, and cannot put up with toil or pleasure or ourselves or anything for long. This weakness has driven some men to their deaths; because by frequently changing their aims they kept falling back on the same things and had left themselves no room for novelty. They began to be sick of life and the world itself, and out of their enervating self-indulgence arose the feeling 'How long must I face the same things?'

You want to know what remedy I can recommend against this boredom. The best course, as Athenodorus says, would be to busy oneself in the practical activity of political involvement and civic duties. For just as some people spend the day in sun-bathing, exercise and the care of their bodies, and for athletes it is of the highest practical importance to spend most of their time cultivating the strength of their limbs, to which alone they have devoted themselves, so for you, who are training your mind for the contests of public life, by far the finest approach is regular practice. For when one intends to make himself useful to his fellow-citizens and fellow-men, he is at the same time getting practice and doing good if he throws himself heart and soul into the duty of looking after both the community and the individual. 'But,' says Athenodorus, 'since mankind is so insanely ambitious and so many false accusers twist right into wrong, making honesty unsafe and bound to meet resistance rather than help, we should indeed retire from public and political life, though a great mind has scope for free activity even in private life. The energies of lions and other animals are restricted by cages, but not of men, whose finest achievements are seen in retirement.

However, let a man seclude himself on condition that, wherever he conceals his leisure, he is prepared to serve both individuals and all mankind by his intellect, his words and his counsel. Service to the state is not restricted to the man who produces candidates for office, defends people in court, and votes for peace and war: the man who teaches the young, who instils virtue into their minds (and we have a great shortage of good teachers), who grips and restrains those who are rushing madly after wealth and luxury, and if nothing more at least delays them – he too is doing a public service, though in private life. Do you imagine that more benefit is provided by the praetors, who settle cases between foreigners and citizens by pronouncing to appellants the verdict of the assessor, than by those who pronounce on the nature of justice, piety, endurance, bravery, contempt of death, knowledge of the gods, and how free a blessing is that of a good conscience? So if you devote to your studies the time you have taken from your public duties you will not have deserted or evaded your task. For the soldier is not only the man who stands in the battle line, defending the right and left wings, but also the one who guards the gates and has the post, less dangerous but not idle, of keeping the watch and guarding the armoury: these duties, though bloodless, count as military service. If you apply yourself to study you will avoid all boredom with life, you will not long for night because you are sick of daylight, you will be neither a burden to yourself nor useless to others, you will attract many to become your friends and the finest people will flock about you. For even obscure virtue is never concealed but gives visible evidence of herself: anyone worthy of her will follow her tracks. But if we shun all society and, abandoning the human race, live for ourselves alone, this isolation, devoid of any interest, will be followed by a dearth of worthwhile activity. We shall begin to put up some buildings, to pull down others, to push back the sea, to draw waters through unnatural channels, and to squander the time which nature gave us to be used. Some of us use it sparingly, others wastefully; some spend it so that we can give an account of it, others so that we have no balance left – a most shameful result. Often a very old man has no other proof of his long life than his age.'

It seems to me, my dear Serenus, that Athenodorus has too easily submitted to the times and too quickly retreated. I would not deny that one has to yield sometimes – but by a gradual retreat, and holding on to our standards and our soldier's honour. Those who are still armed when they agree terms with their enemies are safer and more highly regarded. This, I think, is what Virtue and Virtue's disciple should do: if Fortune gets the better of someone and deprives him of the means of action, he should not immediately turn his back and bolt, dropping his weapons and looking for a place to hide (as if there were any place where Fortune could not find him), but he should apply himself more sparingly to his duties and choose something carefully in which he can serve the state. Suppose he cannot be a soldier: let him seek public office. Suppose he has to live in a private capacity: let him be an advocate. Suppose he is condemned to silence: let him help his fellow-citizens by unspoken support. Suppose it is dangerous for him to be seen in the forum: in private homes, at the shows, at banquets let him play the part of a good companion, a loyal friend, a temperate banqueter. Suppose he has lost the duties of a citizen: let him practise those of a man. With a lofty spirit we have refused to confine ourselves within the walls of one city, and we have gone out to have dealings with the whole earth and claimed the world as our country, for this reason, that we might give our virtue a wider field for action. Suppose you are cut off from judicial office, and public speaking and elections are closed to you: consider all the extensive regions that lie open behind you, all the peoples – you will never find an area barred to you so large that an even larger one is not left open. But take care that this is not entirely your fault – for example, that you don't want to take public office except as consul or prytanis or herald or sufes. But suppose you didn't want to serve in the army except as general or tribune? Even if others hold the front line and your lot has put you in the third rank, you must play the soldier there with your voice, your encouragement, your example and your spirit. Even if a man's hands are cut off, he finds he can yet serve his side by standing firm and cheering them on. You should do something like that: if Fortune has removed you from a leading role in public life you should still stand firm and cheer others on, and if someone grips your throat, still stand firm and help though silent. The service of a good citizen is never useless: being heard and seen, he helps by his expression, a nod of his head, a stubborn silence, even his gait. Just as certain wholesome substances do us good by their odour even without tasting or touching them, so Virtue spreads her advantages even from a distant hiding place. Whether she walks abroad about her legitimate business, or appears on sufferance and is forced to furl her sails, whether she is confined, inactive and dumb, within a narrow space, or fully visible, in any condition at all she does good service. Why do you think that a man living in honourable retirement cannot offer a valuable example? Much the best course, therefore, is to combine leisure with some activity whenever a fully energetic life is impossible owing to the hindrances of chance or the state of the country; for you will never find absolutely every road blocked to some form of honourable activity.

Can you find a more wretched city than Athens when she was being torn apart by the Thirty Tyrants? Having killed thirteen hundred of the best citizens, they did not stop at that, but their very savagery spurred itself on. In a city which contained the Areopagus, a law court of the highest sanctity, and a senate and a popular assembly resembling a senate, there met daily a sinister group of executioners, and the unfortunate senate house was crowded with tyrants. Could that state be at peace where there were as many tyrants as attendants? There could not even be a hope of recovering their liberty nor any obvious chance of retaliation against such powerful villains: for where could the poor country find enough men like Harmodius? Yet Socrates was in the thick of it: he comforted the gloomy city fathers, encouraged those who were despairing of the state, reproached the rich who now feared their own wealth for a tardy repentance of their dangerous greed; and to those willing to imitate him he was a walking inspiration, as he moved about, a free spirit among thirty masters. Yet this was the man that Athens herself put to death in prison, and Freedom could not bear the freedom of the man who had openly scoffed at a whole troop of tyrants. So you can understand both that in a state suffering disaster the wise man has the opportunity to show an influential presence, and that in a successful and prosperous state money-grubbing, envy and a thousand other unmanly vices reign supreme. Therefore, according to the disposition of the state and the liberty Fortune allows us, we shall either extend or contract our activities; but at all events we shall stir ourselves and not be gripped and paralysed by fear. He indeed will prove a man who, threatened by dangers on all sides, with arms and chains clattering around him, will neither endanger nor conceal his courage: for self-preservation does not entail suppressing onself. Truly, I believe, Curius Dentatus used to say that he preferred real death to living death; for the ultimate horror is to leave the number of the living before you die. But if you happen to live at a time when public life is hard to cope with, you will just have to claim more time for leisure and literary work, seek a safe harbour from time to time as if you were on a dangerous voyage, and not wait for public life to dismiss you but voluntarily release yourself from it first.

However, we must take a careful look first at ourselves, then at the activities which we shall be attempting, and then at those for whose sake and with whom we are attempting them.

Above all it is essential to appraise oneself, because we

usually overestimate our capabilities. One man comes to grief through trusting his eloquence; another makes more demands on his fortune than it can stand; another taxes his frail body with laborious work. Some men are too shy for politics, which require a bold appearance; some through brashness are not fitted for court life; some cannot restrain their anger and any feeling of annoyance drives them to reckless language; some cannot control their wit and refrain from smart but dangerous sallies. For all of these retirement is more expedient than public activity: a passionate and impatient nature must avoid provocations to outspokenness that will cause trouble.

Then we must appraise the actual things we are attempting and match our strength to what we are going to undertake. For the performer must always be stronger than his task: loads that are too heavy for the bearer are bound to overwhelm him. Moreover, certain tasks are not so much great as prolific in producing many other tasks: we must avoid those which give birth in turn to new and manifold activities, and not approach something from which we cannot easily withdraw. You must set your hands to tasks which you can finish or at least hope to finish, and avoid those which get bigger as you proceed and do not cease where you had intended.

We must be especially careful in choosing people, and deciding whether they are worth devoting a part of our lives to them, whether the sacrifice of our time makes a difference to them. For some people actually charge us for our services to them. Athenodorus says he would not even go to dinner with a man who did not thereby feel indebted to him. I suppose you realize how much less inclined he was to visit those who repay their friends' services with a meal, and count the courses as largesses, as if they were overdoing the honour paid to another. Take away their witnesses and spectators and there is no fun in private gormandizing.

You must consider whether your nature is more suited to practical activity or to quiet study and reflection, and incline in the direction your natural faculty and disposition take you. Isocrates forcibly pulled Ephorus away from the forum, thinking he would be better employed in writing history. Inborn dispositions do not respond well to compulsion, and we labour in vain against nature's opposition.

But nothing delights the mind so much as fond and loyal friendship. What a blessing it is to have hearts that are ready and willing to receive all your secrets in safety, with whom you are less afraid to share knowledge of something than keep it to yourself, whose conversation soothes your distress, whose advice helps you make up your mind, whose cheerfulness dissolves your sorrow, whose very appearance cheers you up! To be sure, we shall choose those who are as far as possible free from strong desires; for vices spread insidiously, and those nearest to hand are assailed and damaged by contact with them. It follows that, just as at a time of an epidemic disease we must take care not to sit beside people whose bodies are infected with feverish disease because we shall risk ourselves and suffer from their breathing upon us, so in choosing our friends for their characters we shall take care to find those who are the least corrupted:

mixing the sound with the sick is how disease starts. But I am not enjoining upon you to follow and associate with none but a wise man. For where will you find him whom we have been seeking for ages? In place of the ideal we must put up with the least bad. You would scarcely have the opportunity of a happier choice if you were hunting for good men among the Platos and Xenophons and all that offspring of the Socratic breed; or if you had access to the age of Cato, which produced many men worthy to be born in Cato's time. (It also produced many who were worse than at any other time and who committed appalling crimes: for both groups were necessary for Cato to be appreciated – he needed the good to win their approval and the bad to prove his strength.) But in the current dearth of good men you must be less particular in your choice. Still, you must especially avoid those who are gloomy and always lamenting, and who grasp at every pretext for complaint. Though a man's loyalty and kindness may not be in doubt, a companion who is agitated and groaning about everything is an enemy to peace of mind.

Let us turn to private possessions, the greatest source of human misery. For if you compare all the other things from which we suffer, deaths, illnesses, fears, desires, endurance of pains and toils, with the evils which money brings us, the latter will far outweigh the others. So we must bear in mind how much lighter is the pain of not having money than of losing it; and we shall realize that the less poverty has to lose the less agony it can cause us. For you are mistaken if you think that rich people suffer with more fortitude: the pain of a wound is the same in the largest and the smallest bodies. Bion aptly remarks that plucking out hair hurts bald people just as much as those with hair. You can make the same point that rich and poor suffer equal distress: for both groups cling to their money and suffer if it is torn away from them. But, as I said, it is easier to bear and simpler not to acquire than to lose, so you will notice that those people are more cheerful whom Fortune has never favoured than those whom she has deserted. That great-souled man Diogenes realized this, and arranged that nothing could be taken from him. You can call this state poverty, deprivation, need, and give this freedom from care any shameful name you like: I shall not count this man happy if you can find me another who has nothing to lose. If I am not mistaken it is a royal position among all the misers, the cheats, the robbers, the kidnappers, to be the only one who cannot be harmed. If anyone has any doubts about Diogenes' felicity he can also have doubts about the condition of the immortal gods – whether they are living unhappily because they have no estates and parks and costly farms let out to foreign tenants and vast receipts of interest in the forum. Are you not ashamed of yourselves, all of you who are smitten by wealth? Come, look at the heavens: you will see the gods devoid of possessions, and giving everything though they have nothing. Do you think a man who has stripped himself of all the gifts of chance is poor, or that he resembles the immortal gods? Demetrius, Pompey's freedman, was not ashamed to be richer than Pompey: would you say he was thereby happier? He used to keep the tally of his slaves daily like a general reviewing his army, where previously he would have thought it riches to have two under-slaves and a roomier cell. Yet when Diogenes was told that his only slave had run away, he did not think it worth the trouble to get him back. 'It would be degrading,' he said, 'if Manes can live without Diogenes and not Diogenes without Manes.' I think what he meant was: 'Mind your own business, Fortune: Diogenes has nothing of yours now. My slave has run away – no, it is I who have got away free.' A household of slaves needs clothing and food; so many bellies of ravenous creatures must be looked after, garments bought, thieving hands guarded against, and services employed in the face of tears and curses. How much happier is the man who owes nothing to anybody except the one he can most easily refuse, himself! But since we have not such strength of will, we must at least curtail our possessions, so we may be less exposed to the blows of Fortune. Men's bodies are better fitted for warfare if they can be compressed into their armour than if they bulge out of it and by their very bulk are exposed on every side to wounds. So the ideal amount of money is that which neither falls within the range of poverty nor far exceeds it.

Moreover, we shall be satisfied with this limit if we previously practised thrift, without which no amount of wealth is enough, and no amount is not ample enough; especially as a remedy is to hand and poverty can itself turn to riches by practising economy. Let us get used to banishing ostentation, and to measuring things by their qualities of function rather than display. Let food banish hunger and drink banish thirst; let sex indulge its needs;

let us learn to rely on our limbs, and to adjust our style of dress and our way of living not to the newfangled patterns but to the customs of our ancestors. Let us learn to increase our self-restraint, to curb luxury, to moderate ambition, to soften anger, to regard poverty without prejudice, to practise frugality, even if many are ashamed of it, to apply to nature's needs the remedies that are cheaply available, to curb as if in fetters unbridled hopes and a mind obsessed with the future, and to aim to acquire our riches from ourselves rather than from Fortune. It is not possible that all the manifold and unfair disasters of life can be so repelled that many storm winds will not still assail those who spread their sails ambitiously. We must restrict our activities so that Fortune's weapons miss their mark; and for that reason exiles and calamities have proved to benefit us and greater disasters have been mended by lesser ones. When the mind is less amenable to instruction and cannot be cured by milder means, why should it not be helped by having a dose of poverty and disgrace and general ruin – dealing with evil by evil? So let us get used to dining without a mass of people, to being slave to fewer slaves, to acquiring clothes for their proper purpose, and to living in more restricted quarters. Not only in running and the contests of the Circus, but in this race course of our lives we must keep to the inner track.

Even in our studies, where expenditure is most worth while, its justification depends on its moderation. What is the point of having countless books and libraries whose titles the owner could scarcely read through in his whole lifetime? The mass of books burdens the student without instructing him, and it is far better to devote yourself to a few authors than to get lost among many. Forty thousand books were burned in the library at Alexandria. Someone else can praise it as a sumptuous monument to royal wealth, like Titus Livius, who calls it a notable achievement of the good taste and devotion of kings. That was not good taste or devotion but scholarly self-indulgence – in fact, not even scholarly, since they had collected the books not for scholarship but for display. In the same way you will find that many people who lack even elementary culture keep books not as tools of learning but as decoration for their dining-rooms. So we should buy enough books for use, and none just for embellishment. 'But this,' you say, 'is a more honourable expense than squandering money on Corinthian bronzes and on pictures.' But excess in any sphere is reprehensible. How can you excuse a man who collects bookcases of citron-wood and ivory, amasses the works of unknown or third-rate authors, and then sits yawning among all his thousands of books and gets most enjoyment out of the appearance of his volumes and their labels? Thus you will see that the idlest men possess sets of orations and histories, with crates piled up to the ceiling: for nowadays an elegant library too has joined hot and cold baths as an essential adornment for a house. I would certainly excuse people for erring through an excessive love of study; but these collections of works of inspired genius, along with their several portraits, are acquired only for pretentious wall decoration.

But perhaps you have become involved in some difficult situation in life in which either public or private circumstances have fastened a noose on you unawares, which you can neither loosen nor snap. You must reflect that fettered prisoners only at first feel the weight of the shackles on their legs: in time, when they have decided not to struggle against but to bear them, they learn from necessity to endure with fortitude, and from habit to endure with ease. In any situation in life you will find delights and relaxations and pleasures if you are prepared to make light of your troubles and not let them distress you. In no respect has nature put us more in her debt, since, knowing to what sorrows we were born, she contrived habit to soothe our disasters, and so quickly makes us grow used to the worst ills. No one could endure lasting adversity if it continued to have the same force as when it first hit us. We are all tied to Fortune, some by a loose and golden chain, and others by a tight one of baser metal: but what does it matter? We are all held in the same captivity, and those who have bound others are themselves in bonds – unless you think perhaps that the left-hand chain is lighter. One man is bound by high office, another by wealth; good birth weighs down some, and a humble origin others; some bow under the rule of other men and some under their own; some are restricted to one place by exile, others by priesthoods: all life is a servitude. So you have to get used to your circumstances, complain about them as little as possible, and grasp whatever advantage they have to offer: no condition is so bitter that a stable mind cannot find some consolation in it. Often small areas can be skilfully divided up to allow room for many uses and arrangement can make a narrow piece of ground inhabitable. Think your way through difficulties: harsh conditions can be softened, restricted ones can be widened, and heavy ones can weigh less on those who know how to bear them. Moreover, we must not send our desires on a distant hunt, but allow them to explore what is near to hand, since they do not submit to being totally confined. Abandoning those things which are impossible or difficult to attain, let us pursue what is readily available and entices our hopes, yet recognize that all are equally trivial, outwardly varied in appearance but uniformly futile within. And let us not envy those who stand higher than we do: what look like towering heights are precipices. On the other hand, those whom an unfair fate has put in a critical condition will be safer for lowering their pride in things that are in themselves proud and reducing their fortune as far as they can to a humble level. Indeed there are many who are forced to cling to their pinnacle because they cannot descend without falling; but they must bear witness that this in itself is their greatest burden, that they are forced to be a burden to others, and that they are not so much elevated as impaled. By justice, gentleness, kindness and lavish generosity let them prepare many defences against later disasters to give them hope of hanging on more safely. But nothing can rescue us from these mental vacillations so efficiently as always to set some limit to advancements, and not to allow Fortune the decision when they should cease but ourselves to stop far short of that. In this way we shall have some desires to stimulate the mind, but being limited they will not lead us to a state of uncontrolled uncertainty.

What I am saying applies to people who are imperfect, commonplace and unsound, not to the wise man. He does not have to walk nervously or cautiously, for he has such self-confidence that he does not hesitate to make a stand against Fortune and will never give ground to her. He has no reason to fear her, since he regards as held on sufferance not only his goods and possessions and status, but even his body, his eyes and hand, and all that makes life more dear, and his very self; and he lives as though he were lent to himself and bound to return the loan on demand without complaint. Nor is he thereby cheap in his own eyes because he knows he is not his own, but he will act in all things as carefully and meticulously as a devout and holy man guards anything entrusted to him. And whenever he is ordered to repay his debt he will not complain to Fortune, but he will say: 'I thank you for what I have possessed and held. I have looked after your property to my great benefit, but at your command I give and yield it with gratitude and good will. If you want me still to have anything of yours, I shall keep it safe; if you wish otherwise, I give back and restore to you my silver, both coined and plate, my house and my household.' Should Nature demand back what she previously entrusted to us we shall say to her too: 'Take back my spirit in better shape than when you gave it. I do not quibble or hang back: I am willing for you to have straightway what you gave me before I was conscious – take it.' What is the harm in returning to the point whence you came? He will live badly who does not know how to die well. So we must first strip off the value we set on this thing and reckon the breath of life as something cheap. To quote Cicero, we hate gladiators if they are keen to save their life by any means; we favour them if they openly show contempt for it. You must realize that the same thing applies to us: for often the cause of dying is the fear of it. Dame Fortune, who makes sport with us, says, 'Why should I preserve you, base and fearful creature? You will only receive more severe wounds and stabs, as you don't know how to offer your throat. But you will both live longer and die more easily, since you receive the blade bravely, without withdrawing your neck and putting your hands in the way. He who fears death will never do anything worthy of a living man. But he who knows that this was the condition laid down for him at the moment of his conception will live on those terms, and at the same time he will guarantee with a similar strength of mind that no events take him by surprise. For by foreseeing anything that can happen as though it will happen he will soften the onslaught of all his troubles, which present no surprises to those who are ready and waiting for them, but fall heavily on those who are careless in the expectation that all will be well. There is disease, imprisonment, disaster, fire: none of these is unexpected – I did know in what riotous company Nature had enclosed me. So many times have the dead been lamented in my neighbourhood; so many times have torch and taper conducted untimely funerals past my threshold. Often has the crash of a falling building echoed beside me. Many who were linked to me through the forum and the senate and everyday conversation have been carried off in a night, which has severed the hands once joined in friendship.

Should it surprise me if the perils which have always roamed around me should some day reach me? A great number of people plan a sea voyage with no thought of a storm. I shall never be ashamed to go to a bad author for a good quotation. Whenever Publilius abandoned the absurdities of the mime and language aimed at the gallery, he showed more force of intellect than the writers of tragedy and comedy; and he produced many thoughts more striking than those of tragedy, let alone farce, including this one: 'What can happen to one can happen to all.' If you let this idea sink into your vitals, and regard all the ills of other people (of which every day shows an enormous supply) as having a clear path to you too, you will be armed long before you are attacked. It is too late for the mind to equip itself to endure dangers once they are already there. 'I didn't think it would happen' and 'Would you ever have believed it would turn out so?' Why ever not? Are there any riches which are not pursued by poverty and hunger and beggary? What rank is there whose purple robe and augur's staff and patrician shoe-straps are not attended by squalor and the brand of disgrace and a thousand marks of shame and utter contempt? What kingship does not face ruin and trampling down, the tyrant and the hangman? And these things are not separated by wide intervals: there is only a brief hour between sitting on a throne and kneeling to another. Know, then, that every condition can change, and whatever happens to anyone can happen to you too. You are rich: but are you richer than Pompey? Yet even he lacked bread and water when Gaius, his old relation and new host, had opened the house of Caesar to him so that he could close his own. Though he possessed so many rivers flowing from source to mouth in his own lands, he had to beg for drops of water. He died of hunger and thirst in a kinsman's palace, and while he starved his heir was organizing a state funeral for him. You have filled the highest offices: were they as high or unexpected or all-embracing as Sejanus had? Yet on the same day the senate escorted him to prison and the people tore him to pieces; and there was nothing left for the executioner to drag away of the man who had had everything heaped on him that gods and men could offer. You are a king: I shall not direct you to Croesus, who lived to see his own funeral pyre both lit and extinguished, thus surviving not only his kingdom but his own death; nor to Jugurtha, who was put on show to the Roman people within a year of causing them terror. We have seen Ptolemy, king of Africa, and Mithridates, king of Armenia, imprisoned by Gaius. One of them was sent into exile; the other hoped to be sent there in better faith. In all this topsy-turvy succession of events, unless you regard anything that can happen as bound to happen you give adversity a power over you which the man who sees it first can crush.

The next thing to ensure is that we do not waste our energies pointlessly or in pointless activities: that is, not to long either for what we cannot achieve, or for what, once gained, only makes us realize too late and after much exertion the futility of our desires. In other words, let our labour not be in vain and without result, nor the result unworthy of our labour; for usually bitterness follows if either we do not succeed or we are ashamed of succeeding. We must cut down on all this dashing about that a great many people indulge in, as they throng around houses and theatres and fora: they intrude into other people's affairs, always giving the impression of being busy. If you ask one of them as he comes out of a house, 'Where are you going? What do you have in mind?' he will reply, 'I really don't know; but I'll see some people, I'll do something.' They wander around aimlessly looking for employment, and they do not what they intended but what they happen to run across. Their roaming is idle and pointless, like ants crawling over bushes, which purposelessly make their way right up to the topmost branch and then all the way down again. Many people live a life like these creatures, and you could not unjustly call it busy idleness. You will feel sorry for some folk you see rushing along as if to a fire; so often do they bump headlong into those in their way and send themselves and others sprawling, when all the time they have been running to call on someone who will not return the call, or to attend the funeral of somebody they don't know, or the trial of somebody who is constantly involved in litigation, or the betrothal of a woman who is constantly getting married, and while attending a litter have on occasion even carried it. They then return home, worn out to no purpose and swearing they themselves don't know why they went out or where they have been – and the next day they will wander forth on the same old round. So let all your activity be directed to some object, let it have some end in view. It is not industry that makes men restless, but false impressions of things drive them mad. For even madmen need some hope to stir them: the outward show of some object excites them because their deluded mind cannot detect its worthlessness. In the same way every individual among those who wander forth to swell a crowd is led round the city by empty and trivial reasons. Dawn drives him forth with nothing to do, and after he has been jostled in vain on many men's doorsteps and only succeeds in greeting their slave-announcers, shut out by many he finds no one at home with more difficulty than himself. This evil leads in turn to that most disgraceful vice of eavesdropping and prying into public and secret things and learning about many matters which are safe neither to talk about nor to listen to.

I imagine that Democritus had this in mind when he began: 'Anyone who wishes to live a quiet life should not engage in many activities either privately or publicly' – meaning, of course, useless ones. For if they are essential, then not just many but countless things have to be done both privately and publicly. But when no binding duty summons us we must restrain our actions. For a man who is occupied with many things often puts himself into the power of Fortune, whereas the safest policy is rarely to tempt her, though to keep her always in mind and to trust her in nothing. Thus: 'I shall sail unless something happens'; and 'I shall become praetor unless something prevents me'; and 'My business will be successful unless something interferes.' That is why we say that nothing happens to the wise man against his expectation. We remove him not from the chances that befall mankind but from their mistakes, nor do all things turn out for him as he wished but as he reckoned – and above all he reckoned that something could block his plans. But inevitably the mind can cope more easily with the distress arising from disappointed longings if you have not promised it certain success.

We should also make ourselves flexible, so that we do not pin our hopes too much on our set plans, and can move over to those things to which chance has brought us, without dreading a change in either our purpose or our condition, provided that fickleness, that fault most inimical to tranquillity, does not get hold of us. For obstinacy, from which Fortune often extorts something, is bound to bring wretchedness and anxiety, and much more serious is the fickleness that nowhere restrains itself. Both are hostile to tranquillity, and find change impossible and endurance impossible. In any case the mind must be recalled from external objects into itself: it must trust in itself, rejoice in itself, admire its own things; it must withdraw as much as possible from the affairs of others and devote its attention to itself; it must not feel losses and should take a kindly view even of misfortunes. When a shipwreck was reported and he heard that all his possessions had sunk, our founder Zeno said, 'Fortune bids me be a less encumbered philosopher.' When a tyrant threatened to kill the philosopher Theodorus, and indeed to leave him unburied, he replied, 'You can please yourself, and my half-pint of blood is in your power; but as to burial, you are a fool if you think it matters to me whether I rot above or below ground.' Julius Canus, an outstandingly fine man, whom we can admire even though he was born in our age, had a long dispute with Gaius; and as he was going away that Phalaris said to him, 'In case you are deluding yourself with foolish hopes, I have ordered you to be led off to execution.' His reply was 'I thank you, noble emperor.' I am not certain what he meant, for many possibilities occur to me. Did he mean to be insulting by showing the extent of the cruelty which caused death to be a blessing? Was he taunting him with his daily bouts of madness (for people used to thank him whose children had been murdered and whose property had been confiscated)? Was he accepting his sentence as a welcome release? Whatever he meant, it was a spirited reply. Someone will say, 'After this Gaius could have ordered him to live.' Canus was not afraid of that: Gaius was known to keep his word in commands of that sort. Will you believe that Canus spent the ten days leading up to his execution without any anxiety at all? It is incredible what that man said, what he did, how calm he remained. He was playing draughts when the centurion who was dragging off a troop of condemned men ordered him to be summoned too. At the call he counted his pieces and said to his companion, 'See that you don't falsely claim after my death that you won.' Then, nodding to the centurion, he said, 'You will be witness that I am leading by one piece.' Do you think Canus was just enjoying his game at that board? He was enjoying his irony. His friends were sorrowful at the prospect of losing such a man, and he said to them, 'Why are you sad? You are wondering whether souls are immortal: I shall soon know.' He did not cease searching for the truth right up to the end and making his own death a topic for discussion. His philosophy teacher went with him, and when they were not far from the mound on which our god Caesar received his daily offering, he said, 'Canus, what are you thinking about now? What is your state of mind?' Canus replied, 'I have decided to take note whether in that most fleeting moment the spirit is aware of its departure from the body'; and he promised that if he discovered anything he would visit his friends in turn and reveal to them the state of the soul. Just look at that serenity in the midst of a hurricane, that spirit worthy of immortality, which invokes its own fate to establish the truth, and in that very last phase of life questions the departing soul and seeks to learn something not only up to the time of death but from the very experience of death itself. No one ever pursued philosophy longer. So great a man will not quickly be relinquished, and he should be referred to with respect: glorious spirit, who swelled the roll of Gaius' victims, we shall ensure your immortality.

But there is no point in banishing the causes of private sorrow, for sometimes we are gripped by a hatred of the human race. When you consider how rare is simplicity and how unknown is innocence, how you scarcely ever find loyalty except when it is expedient, what a host of successful crimes you come across, and all the things equally hateful that men gain and lose through lust, and how ambition is now so far from setting limits to itself that it acquires a lustre from viciousness – all this drives the mind into a darkness whose shadows overwhelm it, as though those virtues were overturned which it is not possible to hope for and not useful to possess. We must therefore school ourselves to regard all commonly held vices as not hateful but ridiculous, and we should imitate Democritus rather than Heraclitus. For whenever these went out in public, the latter used to weep and the former to laugh; the latter thought all our activities sorrows, the former, follies. So we should make light of all things and endure them with tolerance: it is more civilized to make fun of life than to bewail it. Bear in mind too that he deserves better of the human race as well who laughs at it than he who grieves over it; since the one allows it a fair prospect of hope, while the other stupidly laments over things he cannot hope will be put right. And, all things considered, it is the mark of a greater mind not to restrain laughter than not to restrain tears, since laughter expresses the gentlest of our feelings, and reckons that nothing is great or serious or even wretched in all the trappings of our existence. Let every man contemplate the individual occurrences which bring us joy or grief, and he will learn the truth of Bion's dictum, that all the activities of men are like their beginnings, and their life is not more high-souled or serious than their conception, and that being born from nothing they are reduced to nothing. Yet it is preferable to accept calmly public behaviour and human failings, and not to collapse into either laughter or tears. For to be tormented by other people's troubles means perpetual misery, while to take delight in them is an inhuman pleasure; just as it is an empty show of kindness to weep and assume a solemn look because somebody is burying a son. In your own troubles too, the appropriate conduct is to indulge as much grief as nature, not custom, demands: for many people weep in order to be seen weeping, though their eyes are dry as long as there is nobody looking, since they regard it as bad form not to weep when everyone is weeping. This evil of taking our cue from others has become so deeply ingrained that even that most basic feeling, grief, degenerates into imitation.

We must next look at a category of occurrences which with good reason cause us grief and anxiety. When good men come to a bad end, when Socrates is compelled to die in prison and Rutilius to live in exile, when Pompey and Cicero have to offer their necks to their clients, when Cato, that living pattern of the virtues, has to fall on his sword to show the world what is happening to himself and the state at the same time; then we have to feel anguish that Fortune hands out such unfair rewards. And what can each of us then hope for himself when he sees the best men suffering the worst fates? What follows then? Observe how each of those men bore his fate; and if they were brave, long with your spirit for a spirit like theirs; if they died with womanly cowardice, then nothing died with them. Either they are worthy of your admiration for their courage or unworthy of your longing for their cowardice. For what is more disgraceful than if supremely great men by dying bravely make others fearful? Let us repeatedly praise one who deserves praise and let us say: 'The braver one is, the happier he is! You have escaped all mischances, envy and disease; you have come forth from prison – not that you seemed to the gods worthy of ill fortune, but unworthy that Fortune should any longer have power over you.' But we have to lay hands on those who pull back and at the very point of death look back towards life. I shall weep for no one who is happy and for no one who is weeping: the one has himself wiped away my tears; the other by his own tears has proved himself unworthy of any. Should I weep for Hercules because he was burned alive, or Regulus because he was pierced by all those nails, or Cato because he wounded his own wounds? All of them by giving up a brief spell of time found the way to become eternal, and by dying achieved immortality.

There is also another not inconsiderable source of anxieties, if you are too concerned to assume a pose and do not reveal yourself openly to anyone, like many people whose lives are false and aimed only at outward show. For it is agonizing always to be watching yourself in fear of being caught when your usual mask has slipped. Nor can we ever be carefree when we think that whenever we are observed we are appraised; for many things happen to strip us of our pretensions against our will, and even if all this attention to oneself succeeds, yet the life of those who always live behind a mask is not pleasant or free from care. On the contrary, how full of pleasure is that honest and naturally unadorned simplicity that in no way hides its disposition! Yet this life too runs a risk of being scorned if everything is revealed to everybody; for with some people familiarity breeds contempt. But there is no danger of virtue being held cheap as a result of close observation, and it is better to be despised for simplicity than to suffer agonies from everlasting pretence. Still, let us use moderation here: there is a big difference between living simply and living carelessly.

We should also withdraw a lot into ourselves; for associating with people unlike ourselves upsets a calm disposition, stirs up passions again, and aggravates any mental weakness which has not been completely cured. However, the two things must be mingled and varied, solitude and joining a crowd: the one will make us long for people and the other for ourselves, and each will be a remedy for the other; solitude will cure our distaste for a crowd, and a crowd will cure our boredom with solitude.

The mind should not be kept continuously at the same pitch of concentration, but given amusing diversions. Socrates did not blush to play with small children; Cato soothed his mind with wine when it was tired from the cares of state; and Scipio used to disport that triumphal and military form in the dance, not shuffling about delicately in the present style, when even in walking men mince and wriggle with more than effeminate voluptuousness, but in the old-fashioned, manly style in which men danced at times of games and festivals, without loss of dignity even if their enemies were watching them. Our minds must relax: they will rise better and keener after a rest. Just as you must not force fertile farmland, as uninterrupted productivity will soon exhaust it, so constant effort will sap our mental vigour, while a short period of rest and relaxation will restore our powers. Unremitting effort leads to a kind of mental dullness and lethargy. Nor would men's wishes move so much in this direction if sport and play did not involve a sort of natural pleasure; though repeated indulgence in these will destroy all the gravity and force of our minds. After all, sleep too is essential as a restorative, but if you prolong it constantly day and night it will be death. There is a big difference between slackening your hold on something and severing the link. Law-givers established holidays to give people a public mandate to enjoy themselves, thinking it necessary to introduce a sort of balance into their labours; and, as I said, certain great men gave themselves monthly holidays on fixed days, while others divided every day into periods of leisure and work. I remember that this was the practice of the great orator Asinius Pollio, whom nothing kept at work after the tenth hour. After that time he would not even read his letters, in case something fresh cropped up to be dealt with; but in those two hours he would rid himself of the weariness of the whole day. Some take a break in the middle of the day and keep any less demanding task for the afternoon hours. Our ancestors also forbad any new motion to be introduced in the senate after the tenth hour. The army divides the watches, and those who are returning from an expedition are exempt from night duty. We must indulge the mind and from time to time allow it the leisure which is its food and strength. We must go for walks out of doors, so that the mind can be strengthened and invigorated by a clear sky and plenty of fresh air. At times it will acquire fresh energy from a journey by carriage and a change of scene, or from socializing and drinking freely. Occasionally we should even come to the point of intoxication, sinking into drink but not being totally flooded by it; for it does wash away cares, and stirs the mind to its depths, and heals sorrow just as it heals certain diseases. Liber was not named because he loosens the tongue, but because he liberates the mind from its slavery to cares, emancipates it, invigorates it, and emboldens it for all its undertakings. But there is a healthy moderation in wine, as in liberty. Solon and Arcesilas are thought to have liked their wine, and Cato has been accused of drunkenness; whoever accused him will more easily make the charge honourable than Cato disgraceful. But we must not do this often, in case the mind acquires a bad habit; yet at times it must be stimulated to rejoice without restraint and austere soberness must be banished for a while. For whether we agree with the Greek poet that 'Sometimes it is sweet to be mad,' or with Plato that 'A man sound in mind knocks in vain at the doors of poetry,' or with Aristotle that 'No great intellect has been without a touch of madness,' only a mind that is deeply stirred can utter something noble and beyond the power of others. When it has scorned everyday and commonplace thoughts and risen aloft on the wings of divine inspiration, only then does it sound a note nobler than mortal voice could utter. As long as it remains in its senses it cannot reach any lofty and difficult height: it must desert the usual track and race away, champing the bit and hurrying its driver in its course to a height it would have feared to scale by itself.

So here you have, my dear Serenus, the means of preserving your tranquillity, the means of restoring it, and the means of resisting the faults that creep up on you unawares. But be sure of this, that none of them is strong enough for those who want to preserve such a fragile thing, unless the wavering mind is surrounded by attentive and unceasing care.